Revelation

Revelation

Catherine A. Cory
with Little Rock Scripture Study staff

LITURGICAL PRESS
Collegeville, Minnesota

www.littlerockscripture.org

Cover design by John Vineyard. Interior art by Ned Bustard. Photos and illustrations on pages 19, 33, 43, 58, 69, 89, and 109 courtesy of Getty Images. Map on page 10 created by Ann Blattner.

 This symbol indicates material that was created by Little Rock Scripture Study to supplement the biblical text and commentary. Some of these inserts first appeared in the *Little Rock Catholic Study Bible*; the charts on p. 30 and p. 93 first appeared in the New Collegeville Bible Commentary, *The Book of Revelation*, by Catherine A. Cory; other inserts were created specifically for this book by Michael DiMassa.

Commentary by Catherine A. Cory, © 2006, 2022 by Order of Saint Benedict, Collegeville, Minnesota. Inserts adapted from *Little Rock Catholic Study Bible*, © 2011 by Little Rock Scripture Study, Little Rock, Arkansas; additional inserts, prayers, and study questions by Little Rock Scripture Study staff, © 2022 by Order of Saint Benedict, Collegeville, Minnesota. All rights reserved. No part of this book may be used or reproduced in any manner whatsoever, except brief quotations in reviews, without written permission of Liturgical Press, Saint John's Abbey, PO Box 7500, Collegeville, MN 56321-7500. Printed in the United States of America.

1	2	3	4	5	6	7	8	9

Library of Congress Cataloging-in-Publication Data

Names: Cory, Catherine A., author. | Little Rock Scripture Study Staff, contributor.
Title: Revelation / Catherine A. Cory with Little Rock Scripture Study staff.
Description: Collegeville, Minnesota : Liturgical Press, [2022] | Series: Little Rock scripture study |
   Summary: "A seven-lesson Scripture study on the book of Revelation, including commentary, study and reflection questions, prayers, and access to online lectures"— Provided by publisher.
Identifiers: LCCN 2021036042 (print) | LCCN 2021036043 (ebook) | ISBN 9780814667095 (paperback) |
   ISBN 9780814667101 (epub) | ISBN 9780814667101 (pdf)
Subjects: LCSH: Bible. Revelation—Textbooks.
Classification: LCC BS2825.55 .C67 2022 (print) | LCC BS2825.55 (ebook) | DDC 228/.07—dc23
LC record available at https://lccn.loc.gov/2021036042
LC ebook record available at https://lccn.loc.gov/2021036043

TABLE OF CONTENTS

 Wrap-Up Lectures and Discussion Tips for Facilitators are available for each lesson at no charge. Find them online at LittleRockScripture.org/Lectures/Revelation.

Welcome

The Bible is at the heart of what it means to be a Christian. It is the Spirit-inspired word of God for us. It reveals to us the God who created, redeemed, and guides us still. It speaks to us personally and as a church. It forms the basis of our public liturgical life and our private prayer lives. It urges us to live worthily and justly, to love tenderly and wholeheartedly, and to be a part of building God's kingdom here on earth.

Though it was written a long time ago, in the context of a very different culture, the Bible is no relic of the past. Catholic biblical scholarship is among the best in the world, and in our time and place, we have unprecedented access to it. By making use of solid scholarship, we can discover much about the ancient culture and religious practices that shaped those who wrote the various books of the Bible. With these insights, and by praying with the words of Scripture, we allow the words and images to shape us as disciples. By sharing our journey of faithful listening to God's word with others, we have the opportunity to be stretched in our understanding and to form communities of love and learning. Ultimately, studying and praying with God's word deepens our relationship with Christ.

Revelation

The resource you hold in your hands is divided into seven lessons. Each lesson involves personal prayer and study using this book and the experience of group prayer, discussion, and wrap-up lecture.

If you are using this resource in the context of a small group, we suggest that you meet seven times, discussing one lesson per meeting. Allow about 90 minutes for the small group gathering. Small groups function best with eight to twelve people to ensure good group dynamics and to allow all to participate as they wish.

Some groups choose to have an initial gathering before their regular sessions begin. This allows an opportunity to meet one another, pass out books, and, if desired, view the optional intro lecture for this study available on the "Resources" page of the Little Rock Scripture Study website (www.littlerockscripture.org).

Every Bible study group is a little bit different. Some of our groups like to break each lesson up into two weeks of study so they are reading less each week and have more time to discuss the questions together at their weekly gatherings. If your group wishes to do this, simply agree how much of each lesson will be read each week, and only answer the questions that correspond to the material you read. Wrap-up lectures can then be viewed at the end of every other meeting rather than at the end of every meeting. Of course, this will mean that your study will last longer, and your group will meet more times.

WHAT MATERIALS WILL YOU USE?

The materials in this book include:

- The text of the book of Revelation, using the New American Bible, Revised Edition as the translation.
- Commentary by Catherine A. Cory (which has also been published separately as part of the New Collegeville Bible Commentary series).
- Occasional inserts ⬤ highlighting elements of the chapters of Revelation being studied. Some of these are selected from the *Little Rock Catholic Study Bible* while others are supplied by the author and staff writers.
- Questions for study, reflection, and discussion at the end of each lesson.
- Opening and closing prayers for each lesson, as well as other prayer forms available in the closing pages of the book.

In addition, there are wrap-up lectures available for each lesson. Your group may choose to purchase a DVD containing these lectures or make use of the video lectures available online at no charge. The link to these free lectures is: LittleRockScripture.org/Lectures/Revelation. Of course, if your group has access to qualified speakers, you may choose to have live presentations.

Each person will need a current translation of the Bible. We recommend the *Little Rock Catholic Study Bible*, which makes use of the New American Bible, Revised Edition. Other translations, such as the New Jerusalem Bible or the New Revised Standard Version: Catholic Edition, would also work well.

HOW WILL YOU USE THESE MATERIALS?

Prepare in advance

Using Lesson One as an example:

- Begin with a simple prayer like the one found on page 11.

- Read the assigned material for Lesson One (pages 12–20) so that you are prepared for the weekly small group session.

- Answer the questions, Exploring Lesson One, found at the end of the assigned reading, pages 21–23.

- Use the Closing Prayer on page 24 when you complete your study. This prayer may be used again when you meet with the group.

Meet with your small group

- After introductions and greetings, allow time for prayer (about 5 minutes) as you begin the group session. You may use the prayer on page 11 (also used by individuals in their preparation) or use a prayer of your choosing.

- Spend about 45–50 minutes discussing the responses to the questions that were prepared in advance. You may also develop your discussion further by responding to questions and interests that arise during the discussion and faith-sharing itself.

- Close the discussion and faith-sharing with prayer, about 5–10 minutes. You may use the Closing Prayer at the end of each lesson or one of your choosing at the end of the book. It is important to allow people to pray for personal and community needs and to give thanks for how God is moving in your lives.

- Listen to or view the wrap-up lecture associated with each lesson (15–20 minutes). You may watch the lecture online, use a DVD, or provide a live lecture by a qualified local speaker. View the lecture together at the end of the session or, if your group runs out of time, you may invite group members to watch the lecture on their own time after the discussion.

A note to individuals

- If you are using this resource for individual study, simply move at your own pace. Take as much time as you need to read, study, and pray with the material.

- If you would like to share this experience with others, consider inviting a friend or family member to join you for your next study. Even a small group of two or three provides an opportunity for fruitful dialogue and faith-sharing!

MACEDONIA

ASIA MINOR

Black Sea

Aegean Sea

Pergamum
• Thyatira
  • Sardis
• Smyrna • Philadelphia
  • Ephesus • Laodicea

PATMOS

CRETE

CYPRUS

Mediterranean Sea

0   200 km
0   100 miles

Seven Churches of Revelation

Revelation

LESSON ONE

Introduction and Revelation 1

Begin your personal study and group discussion with a simple and sincere prayer such as:

Prayer

Heavenly Father, you are the Alpha and the Omega, our beginning and end. As we study the revelation given to your servant John, inspire us with hope in your promises and the strength to stay faithful to you always.

Read the Introduction on pages 12–15 and the Bible text of Revelation 1 found in the outside columns of pages 16–19, highlighting what stands out to you.

Read the accompanying commentary to add to your understanding.

Respond to the questions on pages 21–23, Exploring Lesson One.

The Closing Prayer on page 24 is for your personal use and may be used at the end of group discussion.

INTRODUCTION

More than any other part of the New Testament, the book of Revelation evokes greatly varying reactions among its readers. Some find it surreal and confusing and want to ignore it completely. Others find it endlessly fascinating because of its many colorful and sometimes grotesque images. Others, fearful about the future, view the book as an illustrated timeline that will help them better prepare for the events of the end of the world.

But is there more to the book of Revelation? Does Revelation have anything to say to believers who want to read the Scriptures to hear God's voice in the present time, to inspire faith, and challenge themselves and their faith communities to right behavior, now, in the midst of the activities of their everyday lives? To some people's surprise, the answer is yes, provided we seek to understand the book of Revelation from within the social and historical context in which it originated and as the type of literature it is—apocalyptic.

As a first step to reading and interpreting any piece of literature, it is important to learn something about its author and the place and time in which the author wrote. This information helps us determine the author's point of view. We must also take into account any historical circumstances or cultural differences that may have affected his or her approach to the topic. Although Sacred Scripture is different from other literature in the sense that Christians believe it to be inspired of God, its human authors are true authors. Since the word of God is mediated through these human authors' historical and cultural circumstances, we need to ask similar questions about the identity of the biblical author and the place and time in which he lived. Therefore, we will begin this commentary by asking what we know about the author of the book of Revelation and the time and place in which he wrote.

Another thing we need to know when we sit down to read a piece of literature is its genre or literary form. Only then do we know what expectations to have about its meaning. For example, if we know that a particular story is a fable, we can expect to read about talking animals, and we know that we should look for its moral or central teaching. However, we would not expect a fable to give us a scientific study or a lesson in history. Therefore, before beginning our reading of the book of Revelation we also need to ask about its genre.

AUTHORSHIP

The author of the book of Revelation does not tell us much about himself, except that his name was John and that he saw himself as God's servant (1:1). Two early church writers, Justin Martyr (c. A.D. 160) and Irenaeus (c. A.D. 180), associated the author of this book with the apostle John and with the writer of the Fourth Gospel, also known by that name. However, most biblical scholars today think that the author of the book of Revelation was neither an apostle of Jesus nor the author of the Gospel of John. The reasons for this view have to do with differences in the style of writing and the probable date of composition of this book. At most, we can say that the author of the book of Revelation was an early Jewish Christian prophet by the name of John, otherwise unknown in early Christian literature.

DATE OF COMPOSITION AND LOCATION OF THE WORK

John tells his readers that he received the visions about which he writes while residing on Patmos, a small island in the Aegean Sea. Further, he tells us that he was there because he "proclaimed God's word and gave testimony to Jesus" (1:9). Thus we can probably assume that his exile on Patmos came as a result of his preaching activity. He also incorporates letters to seven churches of Asia Minor (modern Turkey) into his work. Therefore, we can locate this work in the eastern Mediterranean (see map on page 10).

Concerning the date of composition of the book of Revelation, the text itself provides few clues. The most important piece of evidence is the author's use of the term "Babylon" for

Rome (18:2). In other Jewish literature written toward the end of the first century A.D., this term is used to describe Rome, but only after the Roman armies had destroyed Jerusalem and the temple in A.D. 70. Recall that the Babylonians had destroyed the Jerusalem temple in the sixth century B.C. and deported the people of Judea, throwing them into the darkest period of their history. Because the book of Revelation also makes this connection between Rome and Babylon, scholars generally agree that was written after A.D. 70. The early church writer Irenaeus suggests that Revelation was written toward the end of Domitian's reign (A.D. 81–96), so, without other evidence to the contrary, a date of A.D. 95–96 is reasonable. This means that the book of Revelation is among the last books to be written in the New Testament. This book was commonly accepted as Sacred Scripture by the latter half of the second century.

THE GENRE OF THE BOOK OF REVELATION

What can we say about the genre of the book of Revelation? John describes his work as a prophecy, even though he never actually calls himself a prophet (1:3). A careful reader of this book will notice right away that we do not have a continuous story as we find in the Gospels. Instead, John records the visions (images) and auditions (voices) that came to him through a divine being, usually an angel. The subject matter of these visions and auditions are "heavenly things" and future events. This kind of work is generally described as an "apocalypse," from a Greek word that means "revelation." In fact, in some Bible translations the book of Revelation is given the title "Apocalypse."

Typical of this genre, the seer (that is, the recipient of the visions) receives revelations through mediation of some sort and then records them in writing. The revelations involve secrets of the cosmos and secrets about the future. Sometimes the seer is allowed to journey to the heavenly locations. Most apocalypses also include a command to the seer to seal up the written account of the visions for some future time.

If we assume that the book of Revelation belongs to the genre "apocalypse," what then are we to understand about its interpretation? Some people read the book of Revelation to find out what will happen when this physical world is destroyed or to discover when it will come to an end—in other words, as a roadmap of the end time. However, we can be quite certain that the author of the book of Revelation did not write it for that purpose and that the original audience did not understand it in that way. Therefore, we would be seriously misled about its meaning if that is what we seek to learn from it today.

Perhaps the best way to understand apocalypses is to investigate the precursors or forerunners of the genre. In recent decades scholars have been debating whether apocalypses have their roots in the writings of the prophets or in Wisdom literature. This question arose out of the fact that one can see features of both genres in a wide variety of Jewish and Christian apocalypses and, in particular, in the book of Revelation.

As mentioned above, John himself describes his book as a prophecy (1:3; 22:7, 10, 18, 19). Nowhere in Revelation does he distinguish Jewish prophets of old from Christian prophets. Therefore, it is reasonable to assume that he understood his prophecy to function in the same way as the prophets before him. Whereas we tend to think of prophets primarily as predictors of the future, the prophets of the Old Testament were better known as spokespersons of God on behalf of the covenant. In that capacity the prophet brought accusations against Israel and Judah when they failed to keep the covenant and warned of God's punishment against wrongdoers. The prophet also brought a message of consolation when, in the midst of their suffering, they thought God had abandoned them or when they repented of their sin. Thus the Old Testament prophets' message was principally a call to conversion and a divine consolation in times of trouble.

Another important aspect of biblical prophecy is its grounding in a particular place and time. In other words, the prophetic author's original, intended meaning is closely connected to the historical circumstances out of which he wrote. For the book of Revelation this means that we ought to read it as a call to conversion and a message of consolation written first for the churches of Asia Minor, in their historical and cultural situation, and now reinterpreted for *our* historical and cultural situation. This is a process that requires prayerful reflection, but it is also in keeping with our understanding of the prophets' role as the conscience of the people.

Other scholars argue that the genre "apocalypse" has its roots in Wisdom literature. The Old Testament books included in this category are Proverbs, Job, and Ecclesiastes, along with Sirach (also known as Ecclesiasticus), and Wisdom of Solomon. While Wisdom literature covers a wide variety of topics, it is principally concerned with questions about universal truth, the meaning of life (and death), and what constitutes human good. As one might expect, then, it also addresses issues of theodicy (response to the problem of evil): Why do the righteous suffer without warrant? Why do the wicked appear to go unpunished? What is the meaning of human suffering, and where is God's justice? All of us can relate to these questions, especially when the difficulties of life become too much to bear.

How have these theodicy questions traditionally been addressed within Judaism and Christianity? Any response must come to terms with two interrelated and sometimes apparently contradictory assertions: God is sovereign (all-powerful and in control) and God is just. If we acknowledge the existence of evil in the world, we are forced to question whether or to what extent God has power over evil. On the other hand, if we assert the sovereignty of God, then we must wonder about God's justice, since experience shows us that evil does indeed go unpunished at times, and good people do suffer harm.

If we accept that the genre of the book of Revelation has roots in Wisdom literature, we can see how it treats questions of theodicy by repeatedly asserting that God is sovereign, reigning supreme not only over the heavenly realm but also over the earthly realm and even the underworld. In addition, it repeatedly asserts that God is just, promising reward to God's holy ones and punishment of the wicked. This message of hope and consolation is especially powerful if the audience for which it is intended is experiencing persecution for its faith.

Finally, as mentioned above, the apocalyptic genre does not presuppose a sustained story line that extends from the beginning to the end of the book. Likewise, the reader of the book of Revelation will observe that the book is not organized chronologically. Rather, its author describes a collection of visions, some of which are situated in the heavenly realm and others on earth; some pertaining to the believing community as it anticipates persecution, others relating to those who have endured the suffering and proved themselves faithful. Often the author will introduce a particular idea or image in an early vision and then return to it later in a series of expanded visions or auditions. For these reasons the reader must resist the temptation to impose a chronology on the book. Any attempt to see the book as a linear map of the events of the end time will necessarily lead to misunderstanding of its message.

To sum up, apocalypses do three things: (1) they console people in situations of persecution; (2) they present a particular interpretation of historical events that focuses on the justice and sovereignty of God and the triumph of good over evil; (3) they persuade their hearers to keep covenant with God, that is, to live in a way that assures that they will be among God's elect in the end time.

Note: This introduction has been abridged from the original introduction to the commentary found in the New Collegeville Bible Commentary, *The Book of Revelation.*

OUTLINE OF THE BOOK OF REVELATION

There are many ways to outline the book of Revelation. Our commentary is organized according to this outline, with additional subdivisions as needed.

I. Rev 1:1-8   Introductory materials

II. Rev 1:9–11:19   First cycle of visions
  A. Rev 1:9-20   Initial vision of one like the son of man
  B. Rev 2:1–3:22   The seven letters to the seven churches of Asia Minor
  C. Rev 4:1–5:14   The vision of God's throne and the Lamb
  D. Rev 6:1–7:17   The opening of the seven seals
  E. Rev 8:1–11:19   The seven trumpets

III. Rev 12:1–20:15   Second cycle of visions
  A. Rev 12:1-18   Vision of the woman and the dragon
  B. Rev 13:1-18   Vision of the beasts of the sea and the land
  C. Rev 14:1-20   Vision of the Lamb and imminent judgment
  D. Rev 15:1–16:21   Visions of the seven bowls
  E. Rev 17:1–18:24   Fall of Babylon (interlude)
  F. Rev 19:1–20:15   Seven visions of the last things

IV. Rev 21:1–22:5   Vision of the New Jerusalem

V. Rev 22:6-21   Concluding materials

I: Prologue

CHAPTER 1

¹The revelation of Jesus Christ, which God gave to him, to show his servants what must happen soon. He made it known by sending his angel to his servant John, ²who gives witness to the word of God and to the testimony of Jesus Christ by reporting what he saw. ³Blessed is the one who reads aloud and blessed are those who listen to this prophetic message and heed what is written in it, for the appointed time is near.

II: Letters to the Churches of Asia

Greeting

⁴John, to the seven churches in Asia: grace to you and peace from him who is and who was and who is to come, and from the seven spirits before his throne, ⁵and from Jesus Christ, the faithful witness, the firstborn of the dead and ruler of the

continue

INTRODUCTORY MATERIALS

Rev 1:1-8

The introductory section of this book consists of a prologue (1:1-3), from which the title of the book is derived, followed by what appears to be the "address" portion of a letter (1:4-8).

1:1-3 Prologue

The first word of the document, *apocalypsis*, means "revelation." Thus the book is known as Revelation or the Apocalypse. The author of the book, who is also the recipient of the revelation, identifies himself as John and describes his purpose in writing: to witness to "the word of God and to the testimony of Jesus Christ" (1:2). He also describes his work as prophecy (1:3). Notice the relationship of parties involved in the transmission of this reve-

lation. The revelation belongs or pertains to Jesus Christ (1:1). It is given by God but is mediated through an angel to John, who in turn reported what he saw to others (the community of believers, 1:1-2). The prologue concludes with a beatitude (a saying that begins, "Blessed is the one . . . ") for those who hear the word and act upon what they hear (1:3). This is a prophet at work, acting as spokesperson for God and calling people to conversion.

 A **beatitude** is a common literary form known as a macarism (from the Greek word *makarios*, meaning "blessed," "fortunate," or "happy") found in ancient literature. In the Old Testament, beatitudes are found most often in liturgical settings (e.g., Pss 33:12; 119:1-2) and in Wisdom literature (e.g., Prov 8:32; Sir 14:1-2). Of course, Jesus' Beatitudes (Matt 5:3-11; Luke 6:20-22) are the best-known examples in the New Testament.

1:4-8 The "address"

This subunit looks like the "address" portion of a letter, but it is somewhat misleading because the letter form is abandoned almost immediately. The author, again identified as John, says that he is writing to the seven churches of Asia. However, he may not have had exactly seven in mind, since seven is a symbolic number representing fullness or perfection. In fact, he may have been referring to *all* the churches of first-century Asia, now Turkey.

 The Hebrew expression "Lord of Hosts" depicts God as the leader of a celestial army (the Hebrew word *sabaoth* means "hosts" or "armies"). The corresponding Greek title, used in Revelation 1:8, is *pantokrator* which means **"almighty."** In Revelation, God's omnipotence (great or unlimited power) is a key theme as the narrative relates God's judgment and just governance of all creation.

kings of the earth. To him who loves us and has freed us from our sins by his blood, 6who has made us into a kingdom, priests for his God and Father, to him be glory and power forever [and ever]. Amen.

> 7Behold, he is coming amid the clouds,
>   and every eye will see him,
>   even those who pierced him.
> All the peoples of the earth will lament him.
>   Yes. Amen.

8"I am the Alpha and the Omega," says the Lord God, "the one who is and who was and who is to come, the almighty."

continue

This opening of the letter contains an extended greeting, beginning with the words "grace to you and peace" (1:4). Notice John's use of patterns of three. This grace and peace has a threefold source: God, the seven spirits before God's throne, and Jesus. Further, God is identified with three tenses of the verb "to be"—"who is and who was and who is to come" (1:4)—an expansion of the divine name "I AM," revealed to Moses at the burning bush (Exod 3:14). Finally, Jesus is described in terms of three roles or functions: "faithful witness, the firstborn of the dead and ruler of the kings of the earth" (1:5). His activities on the community's behalf are also enumerated in a pattern of three: he loves us, freed us from sin, and made us a kingdom and priests of God (1:5-6). In these very succinct statements, John is asserting God's sovereignty, Jesus' triumph over evil and death, and the believers' reason for hope and consolation. As we shall see later, these are the primary elements of John's theodicy (response to the problem of evil).

Finally, the opening of the letter contains a prayerlike expression of confidence in Jesus'

return (1:7). The text of the prayer is constructed of quotations from the Old Testament books of Daniel and Zechariah. Daniel 7:13 describes a vision of "one like a son of man" (a heavenly being who has the appearance of a human) who comes before God's throne in heaven to receive, from God, an everlasting dominion and kingship over all the earth. In the interpretation of Daniel's vision (Dan 7:15-27), this heavenly being is shown to be a symbol of the holy ones of God (Dan 7:18, 22). However, here, in the book of Revelation, the one who will come on the clouds is Jesus Christ.

In Zechariah 12:10 the prophet speaks on behalf of God, saying that God will pour out a spirit of compassion on Judah and Jerusalem, so that they will mourn over the one whom they have pierced. Here, in the book of Revelation, the message continues to be one of hope and consolation, but with an added emphasis on the revelation of Christ as the "pierced" one.

This section ends with a declaration of the sovereignty of God, who is almighty, the beginning and end of all things (1:8). Alpha is the first letter of the Greek alphabet, and Omega is the last.

The First Vision

⁹I, John, your brother, who share with you the distress, the kingdom, and the endurance we have in Jesus, found myself on the island called Patmos because I proclaimed God's word and gave testimony to Jesus. ¹⁰I was caught up in spirit on the Lord's day and heard behind me a voice as loud as a trumpet, ¹¹which said, "Write on a scroll what you see and send it to the seven churches: to Ephesus, Smyrna, Pergamum, Thyatira, Sardis,

continue

FIRST CYCLE OF VISIONS

Rev 1:9–11:19

This first cycle of visions consists of an initial vision (1:9-20) followed by seven letters to the churches of Asia Minor (2:1–3:22), a vision of God's throne and the Lamb (4:1–5:14), the opening of seven seals (6:1–7:17), and the blowing of seven trumpets (8:1–11:19).

INITIAL VISION OF "ONE LIKE A SON OF MAN"

Rev 1:9-20

After the prologue and the opening, John recounts a vision of a heavenly being (1:9-20). He begins by affirming his relationship with his hearers in terms of what they share in Jesus. Again, notice the use of the pattern of three: "I John . . . who share with you the distress, the kingdom, and the endurance we have in Jesus" (1:9). Taken together, these three expressions speak to John's understanding of what it means to participate in the Christian life. The word translated here as "distress" can also mean "persecution" or "tribulation," referring to the end time. The word translated as "kingdom" can also mean "kingly reign" or "sovereignty" and should be taken to refer to the hope the hearers share in the full manifestation of God's power over evil in the end time. Finally, the word "endurance," also translated "patient

endurance," is key to understanding John's message. The word appears seven times in Revelation (1:9; 2:2, 3, 19; 3:10; 13:10; 14:12), and in each case it describes how Christians ought to respond to the troubles they face *because* they are Christian. Later, in 3:10, John is quite explicit that he associates these troubles with the end time.

 Relegation to an island was a common punishment for certain offenses in the Roman Empire. According to Roman law, one could be exiled to an island for promoting what the authorities deemed suspect religious practices or "superstition." **Patmos** was one of several islands in the Aegean Sea where offenders were exiled for this offense (see map on page 10).

Next, John provides the temporal and spatial setting for the vision (1:10-11). The "Lord's day" or "the day (dedicated) to the Lord" is most likely a reference to Sunday, the first day of the week and the day on which early Christians gathered to celebrate Eucharist (see Acts 20:7; 1 Cor 16:2). On this day he was "caught up in spirit," that is, under the influence of the Spirit, perhaps in a trance of some sort, when he heard a great trumpetlike voice. In the first century A.D., the trumpet was used in cultic (worship) settings to signal different elements of the worship service or to announce the beginning of festivals or other public events.

 Trumpets are frequently mentioned in the Old Testament and were utilized for many purposes, both secular and religious. Trumpets were used to announce the arrival of a king (2 Kgs 11:14), to give warning (Num 10:9; 31:6), and to sound the attack before battle (2 Chr 13:14; 1 Macc 4:13). Trumpets were also frequently used for liturgical functions. For example, they announced the

John at Patmos, engraving by Gustave Dore, 1866

beginning of a feast day (Num 10:10) and were sounded during temple sacrifice and at other solemnities (2 Chr 7:6; 29:28; Ezra 3:10). In the New Testament, the trumpet often assumes an eschatological function. In the Gospel of Matthew, Jesus says that a "trumpet blast" will herald the time of the final judgment (24:31), and in 1 Corinthians, Paul writes that "the trumpet will sound" to announce the resurrection of the dead (15:52).

Some biblical scholars have seen in John's description of the setting of his first vision some parallels with the call narratives of the Old Testament prophets (cf. Isa 6; Jer 1; Ezek 1–3). If Revelation 1:9-10 is the setting for John's call to prophesy, then the command to write down the words of the vision and distribute them to seven churches (1:11) describes his first task as prophet. All these churches were located in what is now Turkey.

The vision that follows consists of three parts: the account of the vision itself (1:12-16);

Philadelphia, and Laodicea." ¹²Then I turned to see whose voice it was that spoke to me, and when I turned, I saw seven gold lampstands ¹³and in the midst of the lampstands one like a son of man, wearing an ankle-length robe, with a gold sash around his chest. ¹⁴The hair of his head was as white as white wool or as snow, and his eyes were like a fiery flame. ¹⁵His feet were like polished brass refined in a furnace, and his voice was like the sound of rushing water. ¹⁶In his right hand he held seven stars. A sharp two-edged sword came out of his mouth, and his face shone like the sun at its brightest.

¹⁷When I caught sight of him, I fell down at his feet as though dead. He touched me with his right hand and said, "Do not be afraid. I am the first and the last, ¹⁸the one who lives. Once I was dead, but now I am alive forever and ever. I hold the keys to death and the netherworld. ¹⁹Write down, therefore, what you have seen, and what is happening, and what will happen afterwards. ²⁰This is the secret meaning of the seven stars you saw in my right hand, and of the seven gold lampstands: the seven stars are the angels of the seven churches, and the seven lampstands are the seven churches.

John's response to the vision (1:17-18a); and an interpretation of the vision (1:18b-20). The imagery of the vision is highly symbolic, much of it coming from the writings of Daniel and Ezekiel. The "one like a son of man" (a heavenly being in human form) is an allusion to Daniel 7:13 (see comments on 1:7 above). The mention of his snow-white hair parallels that of the Ancient of Days [God] in Daniel 7:9. Other details of John's description of the heavenly being— dressed in a long robe with a golden sash, with feet that gleamed like polished metal and eyes that blazed like fire (1:13-15)—have parallels with Daniel's vision of a heavenly being in human form who comes to deliver a message about the conflict of nations (Dan 10:5-6).

This description of "one like a son of man" is also reminiscent of Ezekiel's visions of God on the throne. In both cases, what would have been God's torso is said to gleam like amber, and what would have been God's feet has the appearance of fire (see Ezek 1:27; 8:2). Ancient peoples believed that one's power to act resided in the hands and feet and that one's will, intellect, and judgment resided in the eyes and heart. Thus John's heavenly being manifests full power, intellect, and judgment through his unusual feet and eyes (1:14-15).

Finally, the long robe and girdle with which the heavenly being is clothed (1:13) are reminiscent of the dress of the priests of the Jerusalem temple (see Exod 28:4; 39:29; Wis 18:24). Perhaps John is suggesting that this heavenly being has been set apart for some special function in the divine liturgy. This would be consistent with his mention of the trumpet in 1:10. In apocalyptic literature the two-edged sword is a symbol of eschatological (end-time) judgment. The fact that it comes from the heavenly being's mouth means that his *words* are judgment (1:16).

 The resurrected Christ holds the seven stars in his **right hand**, which was the hand traditionally associated with strength and superiority. In the Old Testament, for example, it is the right hand of God that brings victory in battle (Exod 15:6; Pss 44:4; 48:11), and in the New Testament, it is at the right hand of God that the risen Christ is enthroned (Mark 16:19; Heb 1:3).

John's terrified response (1:17) and the consolation that follows (1:17-18) are typical of visions of this sort. See, for example, Daniel's response to the vision of the "man" dressed in linen (Dan 10:8-9) and the heavenly being's words of comfort given in response to his alarm (Dan 10:10-12). In the interpretation of John's vision (1:18-20), the heavenly being reveals himself as the resurrected Christ, the one who was dead but now lives (1:18). The resurrected Christ explains that the seven stars in his hand are the guardian spirits of the seven churches (ancient peoples believed that cities prospered because their guardian angels protected them), and the seven golden lamps are the seven churches (1:20).

The number seven is especially significant here. In Greco-Roman culture the rainbow was thought to consist of seven colors. In the second century A.D., some of the Roman emperors included seven stars on their minted coins as a symbol of world domination. Thus the message of this vision is ultimately one of hope and confidence in the One who possesses power over anything that might affect the churches. Just as the heavenly being in the vision walks among the lamps, the risen Christ continues to dwell among them, and just as he holds the stars in his hand, the risen Christ continues to be responsible for their guardianship.

EXPLORING LESSON ONE

1. What were your impressions of the book of Revelation before you began this study? Did you learn anything in this lesson that changed your understanding of this book?

_____

_____

_____

_____

_____

_____

2. According to the Introduction, what are three purposes of apocalyptic literature?

_____

_____

_____

_____

_____

3. What does the word "apocalypse" mean, and what is the typical subject matter of apocalyptic visions?

_____

_____

_____

_____

_____

4. In the opening verses of Revelation, Jesus is described with a series of three titles (1:5; cf. 3:14). Which of these titles is the most meaningful to you personally? Why?

_____

_____

_____

_____

_____

5. a) Describe the significance that Revelation 1:9 would have had for John's readers.

_____

_____

_____

_____

   b) Specifically, what is the significance of the words "distress," "kingdom," and "endurance" (1:9)?

_____

_____

_____

_____

6. The "one like a son of man" (1:13) symbolizes God in the midst of God's people. Where else in the Old Testament do we find similar symbolic images of God's presence? (See Exod 13:21-22; 19:16-20; Ps 139:7-12; Dan 7:13-14; 10:5-6.)

_____

_____

_____

_____

_____

7. Why does John talk about the eyes, hands, and feet of the figure in his vision (1:14-16)?

_____

_____

_____

_____

_____

8. What does a "two-edged sword" (1:16) symbolize in apocalyptic literature, and when has the word of God been a two-edged sword for you?

_____

_____

_____

_____

_____

9. a) How would the words of Jesus in 1:17-18 give hope to persecuted Christians?

_____

_____

_____

_____

_____

   b) Recall a time when you needed to be reassured that Jesus remains in the world. Was there a prayer, a Scripture verse, or an image that gave you hope?

_____

_____

_____

_____

_____

10. What do the "seven stars" represent (1:20)?

_____

_____

_____

_____

_____

_____

CLOSING PRAYER

Prayer

Blessed is the one who reads aloud and blessed are those who listen to this prophetic message and heed what is written in it . . . (Rev 1:3)

Lord Jesus, you are the faithful witness, the first and the last, the living one. Enlighten our minds and open our hearts so we may understand your word and put into practice the lessons it teaches. Today we pray especially for the grace to . . .

LESSON TWO

Revelation 2–3

Begin your personal study and group discussion with a simple and sincere prayer such as:

Prayer

Heavenly Father, you are the Alpha and the Omega, our beginning and end. As we study the revelation given to your servant John, inspire us with hope in your promises and the strength to stay faithful to you always.

Read the Bible text of Revelation 2–3 found in the outside columns of pages 26–32, highlighting what stands out to you.

Read the accompanying commentary to add to your understanding.

Respond to the questions on pages 34–36, Exploring Lesson Two.

The Closing Prayer on page 37 is for your personal use and may be used at the end of group discussion.

CHAPTER 2

To Ephesus

[1]"To the angel of the church in Ephesus, write this:

"'The one who holds the seven stars in his right hand and walks in the midst of the seven gold lampstands says this: [2]"I know your works, your labor, and your endurance, and that you cannot tolerate the wicked; you have tested those who call themselves apostles but are not, and discovered that they are impostors. [3]Moreover, you have endurance and have suffered for my name, and you have not grown weary. [4]Yet I hold this against

continue

LETTERS TO THE SEVEN CHURCHES

Rev 2:1–3:22

John goes on to record seven letters to the churches of Asia Minor (2:1–3:22). The letters follow a very strict literary pattern, with few variations.

In the opening address of each letter, after the church is identified, the writer describes the source of his prophetic message, namely, the exalted Christ. Notice that almost all the descriptions of Christ are taken from the initial vision, suggesting that we ought to see the letters as part of a larger unit that begins with the vision of "one like a son of man" (1:9-20). In the body of each letter, the church is either consoled on account of the sufferings they endure, or scolded for their offenses against God. In most cases they are both consoled and scolded!

From these letters we can discover what the author thinks are the problems of the churches in his day. Pay careful attention to the section of each letter that begins "Yet I hold this against you . . . " As we read these letters, we might also want to think about whether these problems have any counterpart in the lives of today's faith communities.

The command to listen, which is found in the conclusion of each letter, is typical of prophetic literature. The phrase "to the victor," also in the conclusion of each letter, describes the rewards that faithful ones will receive on account of their devotion to Christ who has conquered; those who shed their blood for the ransom of the saints will be exalted by God (5:5, 9-10). At the conclusion of the book of Revelation, in the vision of the New Jerusalem, we learn that those who conquer (i.e., the victors) will inherit the fullness of covenant relationship with God (cf. 21:7).

What, then, is John doing by including these seven letters in the first major unit of the book of Revelation? On one level he is simply playing the part of a scribe, writing down the words dictated by the exalted Christ. However, we cannot neglect the fact that he is also acting as prophet or spokesperson of God, delivering messages of consolation and warning. In fact, this is the perspective from which the whole of the book of Revelation ought to be read. These are communities that were apparently well known to John and for which he felt responsibility, much as the prophets of the Old Testament felt responsible to call the Israelites to conversion.

2:1-7 Message to the church at Ephesus

Because of its location on the western coast of Asia Minor and at the mouth of the river Cayster, Ephesus was an important commercial center for the eastern part of the Roman Empire in the first century A.D. It was also considered to be among the largest cities of the province, with a population estimated at 250,000. The city played an important role in the life of first-century Judaism and Christianity. The Jewish historian Josephus, for example, notes that there was a substantial Jewish population in Ephesus. The Acts of the Apostles suggests that Paul used Ephesus as his base of operations for two years during his missionary activity (Acts 19:1-41). In addition, early traditions associate John, the author of the Fourth Gospel, with Ephesus. It is also said that Mary, the mother of Jesus, lived there for a time and died at Ephesus.

The city contained shrines in honor of a full range of Greek and Roman deities. Its most important religious site was the temple of Artemis, a Greek mother-goddess and goddess of fertility, which was considered to be one of the Seven Wonders of the World. There was also a 25,000-seat theater in Ephesus. The library of Celsus was located there, along with temples for the imperial cult and shrines of the Egyptian deities. The city had also gained a reputation as a place to study magic, so it was not uncommon to find exorcists there.

In this letter John praises the church at Ephesus for their faithful endurance in the face of deception by false apostles and their heresies (2:2-3). However, he warns them that their initial love (zeal?) has waned, and they are now in danger of losing their faith unless they reform their ways (2:4-5). John's choice of description for the exalted Christ—holding the seven stars and walking among the seven lampstands (see the commentary on 2:1)—is especially appropriate for the church at Ephesus because it was a rich and powerful city, and many biblical scholars think that the church at Ephesus was the mother church of the area. However, John may also want to remind the faithful that the exalted Christ continues to be

you: you have lost the love you had at first. ⁵Realize how far you have fallen. Repent, and do the works you did at first. Otherwise, I will come to you and remove your lampstand from its place, unless you repent. ⁶But you have this in your favor: you hate the works of the Nicolaitans, which I also hate.

⁷"'Whoever has ears ought to hear what the Spirit says to the churches. To the victor I will give the right to eat from the tree of life that is in the garden of God.'"

continue

present among them and therefore knows their deeds, both good and bad.

The promise made to those who conquer (2:7) is reminiscent of the second creation story in Genesis, in which Adam and Eve were barred access to the tree of life after their sin (Gen 3:24). In this letter, those who will be allowed to eat of the tree of life are being restored to an intimate relationship with God such as Adam and Eve enjoyed in paradise. The "tree of life" imagery in Genesis may have been introduced here as a counterpoint to the sacred tree of the cult of Artemis.

The city of Ephesus's great theater and the devotion of the Ephesians to the goddess Artemis both play an important role in the story of **Paul's mission** to the city in Acts 19:23-40.

2:8-11 Message to the church at Smyrna

The city of Smyrna was located on the western coast of Asia Minor, north of Ephesus. It had a good harbor, and its location at the end of a major east-west road made it an important commercial city in the first century A.D., though its origins date back to 1000 B.C. Along with Ephesus, Sardis, and Pergamum, it was one of four centers of the provincial assembly of Asia

To Smyrna

[8]"To the angel of the church in Smyrna, write this:

"'The first and the last, who once died but came to life, says this: [9]"I know your tribulation and poverty, but you are rich. I know the slander of those who claim to be Jews and are not, but rather are members of the assembly of Satan. [10]Do not be afraid of anything that you are going to suffer. Indeed, the devil will throw some of you into prison, that you may be tested, and you will face an ordeal for ten days. Remain faithful until death, and I will give you the crown of life.

[11]"'"Whoever has ears ought to hear what the Spirit says to the churches. The victor shall not be harmed by the second death."'

To Pergamum

[12]"To the angel of the church in Pergamum, write this:

"'The one with the sharp two-edged sword says this: [13]"I know that you live where Satan's throne is, and yet you hold fast to my name and have not denied your faith in me, not even in the days of Antipas, my faithful witness, who was martyred among you, where Satan lives. [14]Yet I have a few things against you. You have some people there who hold to the teaching of Balaam, who instructed Balak to put a stumbling block before the Israelites: to eat food sacrificed to idols and

continue

Minor and the first in the province to build a temple to the goddess Roma (Rome). In A.D. 26 the city built a temple to Tiberius, making it second only to Pergamum as a center for the emperor cult (worship of the emperor as a manifestation of the Roman deities). Although we know relatively little about life in Smyrna in the first century, evidence from the second century indicates that the city was suffering under many conflicts—between Christians and non-Christians, between rich and poor, and between local government authorities and

28

Roman provincial authorities. Bishop Polycarp was martyred at Smyrna in A.D. 155.

This letter differs from the form outlined above in that there is no accusation of the community, presumably because the author has nothing with which to charge them. He acknowledges their economic poverty, calling them rich, presumably rich in faith (2:9). Further, he encourages them to stand firm in the face of persecution and not to fear the suffering that is about to befall them (2:10). They will be arrested, he says, and some will even be put to death, but those who are faithful to the end will survive the "test[ing]" and will be rewarded with eternal life. Thus the description of the exalted Christ as the one who "once died but came to life" (2:8) is consistent with John's expectations for the future of the community at Smyrna.

The source of the Christian community's persecution appears to have been the Jewish synagogue ("assembly") in Smyrna (2:9), further suggesting an intra-family fight between Jews and Christian Jews, that is, Jews who accepted Jesus as the messiah. The ten days of tribulation (2:10) may be an allusion to the story of Daniel and his friends, who were tested for ten days when they refused to eat the king's food, which had been dedicated to idols (Dan 1:12-15; cf. 5:3-4). The promise that those who conquer will escape the "second death" (2:11) is a reference to final judgment (see 20:11-15).

2:12-17 Message to the church at Pergamum

Like many of the major cities in Asia Minor, Pergamum's history is very long. During the Hellenistic period, in the early third century B.C., it became famous as the capital of an independent kingdom in western Asia Minor. However, on the death of its last king, King Attalus III, in 133 B.C., the kingdom was bequeathed to the Romans, and shortly after that time Pergamum became the capital of the Roman province of Asia Minor. During the reign of the Roman emperor Augustus (31 B.C.–A.D. 14), the province was reconstituted, and perhaps at that time Ephesus became its capital, but Pergamum likely retained some of its special status for imperial authorities, being the first to build a temple to Augustus.

Throughout this period the city of Pergamum was known as an important center of learning, having one of the largest libraries in the world, and a center for the arts, including a famous school of sculpture. Pergamum also possessed a sanctuary of Asclepius, a Greek god of healing, where people could obtain medical care and where they studied rhetoric. The famous medical doctor Galen was from Pergamum. Temples to several other deities were located here, including a temple to Zeus, the highest deity in the Roman pantheon. The city was also known for its silver mines and for the making of textiles and parchment. Agricultural work flourished here as well.

In this letter the exalted Christ is described as having a sharp, two-edged sword, suggesting judgment, either of the Christian community or of the city itself (2:12; cf. Isa 11:4; 49:2). The author of the letter begins by acknowledging the difficult situation of the community: they live in the place where Satan has his throne (2:13). This is likely a reference to the position of esteem that Pergamum held in the emperor cult and in the worship of Roman deities. It is interesting to note that the previous letter calls the synagogue at Smyrna the "assembly of Satan" (2:9), suggesting some kind of collusion between the Roman authorities and the synagogue. Here, too, the Christian community is praised for standing firm in the face of persecution (2:13).

However, all is *not* well. John accuses the Christian community of harboring some who teach that it is permissible to compromise their faith and participate in idol worship (2:14). (For the story of Balak and Balaam, see Num 22:1–24:25.) They also tolerate the teachings of the Nicolaitans, who apparently hold a similar view on participating in pagan cults (2:15; 2:6). In other words, they have accommodated the practice of their faith to the demands of the wider culture to such an extent that they have compromised the integrity of their faith. Needless to say, the author of the letter considers this to

to play the harlot. ¹⁵Likewise, you also have some people who hold to the teaching of [the] Nicolaitans. ¹⁶Therefore, repent. Otherwise, I will come to you quickly and wage war against them with the sword of my mouth.

¹⁷"'Whoever has ears ought to hear what the Spirit says to the churches. To the victor I shall give some of the hidden manna; I shall also give a white amulet upon which is inscribed a new name, which no one knows except the one who receives it.'"

To Thyatira

¹⁸"To the angel of the church in Thyatira, write this:

be a very serious problem! Hence the description of the exalted Christ as having a sharp, two-edged sword, the symbol of judgment (2:12).

The promise made to the ones who conquer (2:17) has messianic and salvific overtones. Jewish apocalyptic literature describes an expectation that the manna of the Exodus will return in the messianic age. The meaning of the white stone (2:17) likely has something to do with victory, and the new name signals a new destiny or a new way of life.

 The **change in name** promised to those in Pergamum who persevere in their faith follows a biblical tradition of renaming individuals in order to mark a significant change in their spiritual situation or their relationship with God. Examples of such renaming include Abram/Abraham (Gen 17:5), Sarai/Sarah (Gen 17:15), Jacob/Israel (Gen 32:29), and Simon/Peter (John 1:42).

2:18-29 Message to the church at Thyatira

The city of Thyatira was located in Lydia in the western part of Asia Minor. Although few

"'The Son of God, whose eyes are like a fiery flame and whose feet are like polished brass, says this: ¹⁹"I know your works, your love, faith, service, and endurance, and that your last works are greater than the first. ²⁰Yet I hold this against you, that you tolerate the woman Jezebel, who calls herself a prophetess, who teaches and misleads my servants to play the harlot and to eat food sacrificed to idols. ²¹I have given her time to repent, but she refuses to repent of her harlotry. ²²So I will cast her on a sickbed and plunge those who commit adultery with her into intense suffering unless they repent of her works. ²³I will also put her children to death. Thus shall all the churches come to know that I am the searcher of hearts and minds and that I will give each of you what your works deserve. ²⁴But I say to the rest of you in Thyatira, who do not uphold this teaching and know nothing of the so-called deep secrets of Satan: on you I will place no further burden, ²⁵except that you must hold fast to what you have until I come.

²⁶"'To the victor, who keeps to my ways
until the end,
I will give authority over the nations.
²⁷He will rule them with an iron rod.
Like clay vessels will they be smashed,

²⁸just as I received authority from my Father. And to him I will give the morning star.

²⁹"'Whoever has ears ought to hear what the Spirit says to the churches.'"

continue

artifacts remain today, the city is believed to have played an important role in the civic life of the area from the second century B.C. through the third century A.D. Apparently it was also an important center for the making and trading of wool. The Acts of the Apostles tells a story about a woman named Lydia, who was from Thyatira and was baptized by Paul after listening to his preaching (Acts 16:11-15). Lydia was a dealer in expensive purple dyes. Like several of its neighbors, Thyatira had religious sites associated with the emperor cult and shrines to the Greek and Roman deities.

 Like numbers (see chart on page 93), the **colors** used throughout the book of Revelation are symbolic. While the context often helps us understand their significance, this list of color symbols provides basic meanings.

Color	Significance
White	Victory, triumph
Red	Bloodshed, violence
Scarlet	Royalty, bloodshed
Purple	Royalty
Black	Famine
Pale green	Death

In this letter the exalted Christ is described as the Son of God, with eyes of fire and shining feet (2:18), perhaps in contrast to the sun god Helius, whose devotees had a shrine in Thyatira. The members of the Christian community are praised for their love, above all, and for the fact that they continue to grow in holiness (2:19). However, they are scolded for enduring the influence of a prophetess who deceives people and lures them into idolatry (2:20). It is likely that she is a Nicolaitan (see 2:12-17). The name Jezebel is a reference to a Canaanite queen of King Ahab, who established the cult of Baal (worship of any of various local fertility or nature gods among Semitic peoples) in Israel and doomed Ahab's dynasty (2 Kgs 10:1-12). Fornication and adultery should be understood metaphorically to describe participation in idol worship.

Finally, a double promise is made to the victors (2:26-28). First, they will be given authority over the nations, an allusion to Psalm 2, which, already by the first century B.C., was thought to refer to the Jewish messiah. Second, they will be given the morning star. The meaning of the latter is uncertain.

3:1-6 Message to the church at Sardis

Sardis was located in Asia Minor, approximately sixty miles inland from Smyrna and Ephesus. Along with Ephesus, Smyrna, and Pergamum, it was one of four centers of the Roman provincial assembly of Asia and the regional capital of Lydia. The Jewish historian Josephus mentions the existence of a large Jewish community there in the first century A.D. However, we know little about the Christian community in Sardis until the second century, and then primarily through the writings of Melito, the bishop of Sardis. Apparently, persecutions of Christians were conducted in Sardis during that period. The city was founded in the third century B.C.

In this letter the description of the exalted Christ appears to build upon the mention of the morning star at the end of the previous letter, but like the other letters, it also includes details from the initial vision of "one like a son of man" (3:1; see 1:16, 20). Again, like the earlier letters, the author begins, "I know your works . . . " (3:1). However, he has nothing positive to say about this community. They may have a reputation of goodness, but they are in fact as good as dead! Thus he tells them that they better wake up and strengthen what still survives of their faith (3:2). If they do not, he will come when they least expect and inflict judgment on them (3:3).

The promise to the victors is a robe of victory (3:4-5; see chart on the symbolism of colors on p. 30) and assurance that their names will always be found in the book of life (3:5), an allusion to the book of names of the holy ones in 20:12.

The **book of life**, a heavenly "registry" of those who are righteous, is mentioned several times in the Old Testament (Exod 32:32-33; Ps 139:16; Isa 4:3; Dan 12:1; Mal 3:16). In Revelation, the names included in the book of life have been there "from the foundation of the world" and identify those righteous ones who persevere in faith to the end (17:8; 20:15).

CHAPTER 3

To Sardis

[1]"To the angel of the church in Sardis, write this:

"'The one who has the seven spirits of God and the seven stars says this: "I know your works, that you have the reputation of being alive, but you are dead. [2]Be watchful and strengthen what is left, which is going to die, for I have not found your works complete in the sight of my God. [3]Remember then how you accepted and heard; keep it, and repent. If you are not watchful, I will come like a thief, and you will never know at what hour I will come upon you. [4]However, you have a few people in Sardis who have not soiled their garments; they will walk with me dressed in white, because they are worthy.

[5]"'"The victor will thus be dressed in white, and I will never erase his name from the book of life but will acknowledge his name in the presence of my Father and of his angels.

[6]"'"Whoever has ears ought to hear what the Spirit says to the churches."'

To Philadelphia

[7]"To the angel of the church in Philadelphia, write this:

"'The holy one, the true,
who holds the key of David,
who opens and no one shall close,
who closes and no one shall open,

says this:
[8]"'"I know your works (behold, I have left an open door before you, which no one can close). You have limited strength, and yet you have kept

continue

3:7-13 Message to the church at Philadelphia

Philadelphia was located in western Asia Minor, along a route between Smyrna and Sardis. The city was founded in the second century my word and have not denied my name. ⁹Behold, I will make those of the assembly of Satan who claim to be Jews and are not, but are lying, behold I will make them come and fall prostrate at your feet, and they will realize that I love you. ¹⁰Because you have kept my message of endurance, I will keep you safe in the time of trial that is going to come to the whole world to test the inhabitants of the earth. ¹¹I am coming quickly. Hold fast to what you have, so that no one may take your crown.

¹²"'The victor I will make into a pillar in the temple of my God, and he will never leave it again. On him I will inscribe the name of my God and the name of the city of my God, the new Jerusalem, which comes down out of heaven from my God, as well as my new name.

¹³"'Whoever has ears ought to hear what the Spirit says to the churches.'"

To Laodicea

¹⁴"To the angel of the church in Laodicea, write this:

"'The Amen, the faithful and true witness, the source of God's creation, says this: ¹⁵"I know your works; I know that you are neither cold nor hot. I wish you were either cold or hot. ¹⁶So, because you are lukewarm, neither hot nor cold, I will spit you out of my mouth. ¹⁷For you say, 'I am rich and affluent and have no need of anything,' and yet do not realize that you are wretched, pitiable, poor, blind, and naked. ¹⁸I advise you to buy from me gold refined by fire so that you may be rich, and white garments to put on so that your shameful nakedness may not be exposed, and buy ointment to smear on your eyes so that you may see. ¹⁹Those whom I love, I reprove and chastise. Be earnest, therefore, and repent.

²⁰"'Behold, I stand at the door and knock. If anyone hears my voice and opens the door, [then] I will enter his house and dine with him, and he with me. ²¹I will give the victor the right to sit with me on my throne, as I myself first won the victory and sit with my Father on his throne.

²²"'Whoever has ears ought to hear what the Spirit says to the churches.'"'"

B.C. by one of the kings of Pergamum, when the area was still an independent kingdom. Because of the fertile farmland around it, Philadelphia became a center of agriculture, as well as leather working and textile making. However, the area was also prone to earthquakes, and Philadelphia was hit especially hard in the early part of the first century, leaving significant damage to city buildings and walls. It suffered another setback when, in A.D. 92, during the reign of Domitian, the provinces were ordered to destroy half of their vineyards and were not allowed to plant new ones. This city's most important deity was Dionysius, the god of wine. Some from among the Christian community at Philadelphia were martyred along with Polycarp at Smyrna in A.D. 155.

Breaking with the pattern of the previous letters, the description of the exalted Christ in the letter to the Philadelphians does not go back to the initial vision of "one like a son of man," except for the mention of keys (3:7; cf. 1:18). Here the key is the key of David, suggesting authority that is granted them because of their faith in the messiah of the Jews. The open door is a metaphor for opportunity (3:8). The writer acknowledges that the community has little power right now, but he tells them that eventually their opponents—the "assembly (synagogue) of Satan" is a derogatory reference to the Jewish community at Philadelphia—will come to their way of thinking (3:9).

Although hinted at in other letters, here the theme of theodicy is made explicit: God will vindicate the righteous and make the wicked see the error of their ways. The promise given to this community is an anticipation of the final vision of the book of Revelation, the New Jerusalem (3:12). As we shall see later, the New Jerusalem will have no need of a temple because the whole city and its inhabitants will constitute the temple of God and the Lamb (see 21:2, 22-23).

3:14-22 Message to the church at Laodicea

Located southeast of Philadelphia, Laodicea was a major commercial city in the first century A.D. Because it was not far from Hierapolis, the waterfall that emptied out of the hot springs of that city apparently could be seen in Laodicea. It had been founded during the reign of the Greek king Antiochus II (261–246 B.C.) and, under Roman rule, had grown into a manufacturing center for clothing and carpets made from a special type of black wool produced in the area. Laodicea boasted a medical school known for the healing of eye diseases, and it served as a major banking center. The city itself was very wealthy, as evidenced by the fact that it rebuilt quickly and without aid from outside sources after a devastating earthquake in A.D. 60.

In the opening of this letter, the exalted Christ is given three attributions, none of which is connected to the initial vision of the "one like a son of man" (3:14; see 1:9-20). Here we find the only reference in the New Testament to Christ as the "Amen," meaning "So be it." This attribution suggests a position of great authority, much like the third attribution, "source of God's creation" (3:14). The Greek word *archē*, here translated as "source," can also mean "ruler" or "beginning." The second attribution, "faithful and true witness," recalls 1:5 and anticipates 19:11, where Christ is similarly described.

Unlike most of the other letters, the phrase "I know your works" (3:15) is not an introduction to praise or consolation, but rather an indictment. Using the imagery of water, perhaps the now tepid, sulfurous water descending from the hot springs at Hierapolis, the writer says he is about to spit them out of his mouth because, comfortable in their riches, they are disgustingly lukewarm in their faith (3:15-17). Worse yet, they have deluded themselves into thinking that they are among the spiritual elite, people of admirable faith (3:17). This letter, then, is intended as a rude awakening to the church at Laodicea!

With an ironic twist, the message quickly turns to consolation. Their spiritual poverty will be remedied by a gift of fire-refined gold (3:18), an Old Testament image for the purifying effects of suffering (Mal 3:2). They will be relieved of their nakedness with garments of

victory, the reward of the martyrs, and they will be given new sight through the saving ointment that Jesus brings (3:18). Recall that these are the things for which this city is renowned: riches, fine clothing, and medicine for eyes. Again the author draws upon the image of an open door—opportunity—and promises that anyone who opens to Jesus will dine with him, a clear allusion to Eucharist (3:20). Finally, the victor is promised a seat on God's throne (3:21). We will return to both of these images—the open door and the throne of God—in the next section of this book.

Prayer starter: Picture Christ standing at a closed door, knocking (Rev 3:20). That loving invitation has not changed over the ages. Listen carefully for that knock—whether it is faint and gentle or loud and insistent. It is never too late to open the door and have supper with the Lord.

Jesus knocking (Rev 3:20)

EXPLORING LESSON TWO

1. According to the commentary, what are some likely reasons the church at Ephesus is the first church John addresses?

_____

_____

_____

_____

_____

2. a) List the positive qualities John (speaking on behalf of the exalted Christ) finds in the Ephesian Christian community (2:2-3).

_____

_____

_____

_____

   b) Which of these qualities could be applied to your parish or community? Give an example.

_____

_____

_____

_____

3. Why would Christ's promise of "the right to eat from the tree of life" be especially appealing in Ephesus (2:7)? (See Gen 2:9.)

_____

_____

_____

_____

_____

4. a) How can Christians in Smyrna be both poor and rich (2:9)? (See Ps 9:19; 72:12-13; Jas 2:5.)

_____

_____

_____

_____

b) Recall someone you know who has little and yet seems secure and at peace. What brings them security?

_____

_____

_____

_____

5. a) What conflicts may have been going on in Smyrna (2:8-10)?

_____

_____

_____

_____

b) In what ways do Christians face these types of conflicts today, and how can we respond?

_____

_____

_____

_____

6. John (speaking on behalf of Christ) appears not to be fooled by the good reputation of Sardis. How can a Christian community look good on the outside but really be "dead" (3:1)? (See Heb 3:12-14; Jas 2:14-17.)

_____

_____

_____

_____

7. What does the color white symbolize, and how is it used in Revelation to describe objects, persons, and clothing (3:4-5)? (See 2:17; 3:18; 7:13-14; 19:11-14.)

_____

_____

_____

_____

_____

8. John (speaking on behalf of Christ) used a natural phenomenon to warn against spiritual mediocrity (3:15-16). Are there distractions or other factors that can pull you into lukewarmness? How do you deal with these challenges?

_____

_____

_____

_____

_____

_____

9. The Laodiceans' wealth led them to believe they were spiritually elite. Why is this attitude so dangerous? (See Matt 6:1-4, 19-21; 11:29; 23:12; Mark 2:16-17.)

_____

_____

_____

_____

_____

_____

10. Recall the three goals of apocalyptic literature (see Introduction). Then review the seven letters in Revelation 2–3, and find a verse or two that represents each of these goals.

_____

_____

_____

_____

_____

_____

CLOSING PRAYER

Prayer

"Remain faithful until death, and I will give you the crown of life." (Rev 2:10)

Jesus, the holy one, the true, we are weak, and there are so many distractions in the world that can draw us away from you! Grant us the grace to persevere in our faith despite all challenges and temptations. Help us today and every day to disregard whatever would separate us from you, especially . . .

LESSON THREE

Revelation 4–7

Begin your personal study and group discussion with a simple and sincere prayer such as:

Prayer

> *Heavenly Father, you are the Alpha and the Omega, our beginning and end. As we study the revelation given to your servant John, inspire us with hope in your promises and the strength to stay faithful to you always.*

Read the Bible text of Revelation 4–7 found in the outside columns of pages 40–48, highlighting what stands out to you.

Read the accompanying commentary to add to your understanding.

Respond to the questions on pages 49–51, Exploring Lesson Three.

The Closing Prayer on page 52 is for your personal use and may be used at the end of group discussion.

III: God and the Lamb in Heaven

CHAPTER 4

Vision of Heavenly Worship

[1]After this I had a vision of an open door to heaven, and I heard the trumpetlike voice that had spoken to me before, saying, "Come up here and I will show you what must happen afterwards." [2]At once I was caught up in spirit. A throne was there in heaven, and on the throne sat [3]one whose appearance sparkled like jasper and carnelian. Around the throne was a halo as brilliant as an emerald. [4]Surrounding the throne I saw twenty-four other thrones on which twenty-four elders sat, dressed in white garments and with gold crowns on their heads. [5]From the throne came flashes of lightning, rumblings, and peals of thunder. Seven flaming torches burned in front of the throne, which are the seven spirits of God. [6]In front of the throne was something that resembled a sea of glass like crystal.

In the center and around the throne, there were four living creatures covered with eyes in front and in back. [7]The first creature resembled a

continue

THE VISION OF GOD'S THRONE AND THE LAMB

Rev 4:1–5:14

There are several types of visions in the book of Revelation. This vision is a theophany, that is, a revelation or manifestation of God. The Greek word *theos* means "God." Typically, theophanies have a mountain setting. The seer (i.e., the recipient of the vision) is taken to, or otherwise allowed to see, where God resides. The vision is accompanied by heavenly voices and cosmic manifestations of the power of God, like lightning, fire, and thunder. The seer usually describes himself as being in a trance, and time appears to stand still, at least momentarily. In this theophany John sees an open door and is told, "Come up here . . ." (4:1; see 3:20).

The throne that John is allowed to see derives its imagery from the Hellenistic royal court. Hence the description of the immense throne at the end of the throne room and the floor that looked like a sea of glass (4:2, 6). In ancient cultures the throne was the symbol of the king's authority. Therefore, the more intimidating it was, the more it said about the king's authority. Interestingly, in this vision the one seated on the throne (4:3) is described, not in anthropomorphic terms, as one might expect, but by analogy to precious stones, perhaps to suggest that God's kingly splendor surpasses that of any earthly king.

The identity of the twenty-four elders (4:4) is unknown, though scholars have suggested that they represent the sum of the twelve tribes of Israel and the twelve apostles. The same two groups appear together in the final vision of the New Jerusalem in Revelation 21–22. Twenty-four, being a multiple of twelve, represents fullness or perfection. They are dressed in white, symbolizing victory, and they wear crowns of gold, symbolizing their royal authority (4:4). The seven spirits of God are the angels of the presence, who stand before God's throne (4:5).

The "four living creatures" (4:6) are called watchers, or *merkabah* angels, in the Jewish hierarchy of angels. These watchers are sometimes portrayed as angels of fire who support

God's throne or as heavenly beings covered with eyes, with which they constantly keep watch over the throne. The notion probably originated with the Jewish idea of the cherubim, who were part of the throne of the ark of the covenant in the holy of holies. In distinguishing these watchers as the four different animal creatures (4:7-8), John most likely was influenced by Ezekiel 1:5-14. In later Christian theology the symbols of the four living creatures become associated with the four Gospels: the lion (Mark), the ox (Luke), the man (Matthew), and the eagle (John).

In the Hebrew language, words or numbers repeated three times in a row express the highest degree of something. Thus the phrase **"Holy, holy, holy"** (Rev 4:8) means "holiest." This exclamation of the four living creatures is an echo from the call scene of Isaiah, where the angelic choruses are described as giving the highest praise to God as Lord of the universe (Isa 6:2-3). The church prays these words at every Mass to praise and honor God.

The watchers' prayer of praise recalls the description of God in the opening of the book of Revelation: "The Lord God almighty, / who was, and who is, and who is to come" (4:8; cf. 1:8). Each time the watchers give glory to God, the twenty-four elders bow down in homage to God (4:10). The casting down of their crowns (4:10) is similar to Hellenistic oriental kingship rituals in which vassal kings cast their crowns at the emperor's feet to declare their allegiance and identify themselves as the emperor's vassals. The proclamation, "Worthy are you" (4:11), was the standard way that the Roman emperor was addressed as he entered the throne room. All this is to say that John's audience would have readily understood the message of this vision: God is, always was, and always will be all-powerful and king over all that exists.

lion, the second was like a calf, the third had a face like that of a human being, and the fourth looked like an eagle in flight. [8]The four living creatures, each of them with six wings, were covered with eyes inside and out. Day and night they do not stop exclaiming:

"Holy, holy, holy is the Lord God almighty,
    who was, and who is, and who is to come."

[9]Whenever the living creatures give glory and honor and thanks to the one who sits on the throne, who lives forever and ever, [10]the twenty-four elders fall down before the one who sits on the throne and worship him, who lives forever and ever. They throw down their crowns before the throne, exclaiming:

[11]"Worthy are you, Lord our God,
    to receive glory and honor and power,
for you created all things;
    because of your will they came to be and
        were created."

continue

Tuesday evening prayer in the church's Liturgy of the Hours combines three canticles from Revelation 4–5 to form one hymn of praise. The **three canticles** begin "Worthy are you, Lord our God" (4:11), "Worthy are you to receive the scroll" (5:9), and "Worthy is the Lamb that was slain" (5:12).

John signals a new scene in his vision of the heavenly throne room when he says, "[Then] I saw . . ."(5:1). The first scene shows that God is sovereign; this second scene will address the question of God's justice. The description of the One on the throne holding a scroll (5:1) resembles depictions of the Roman emperor seated on his throne as judge and holding a *libellus*, a petition or letter in the form of an open scroll. The seer, John, first experiences

CHAPTER 5

The Scroll and the Lamb

[1]I saw a scroll in the right hand of the one who sat on the throne. It had writing on both sides and was sealed with seven seals. [2]Then I saw a mighty angel who proclaimed in a loud voice, "Who is worthy to open the scroll and break its seals?" [3]But no one in heaven or on earth or under the earth was able to open the scroll or to examine it. [4]I shed many tears because no one was found worthy to open the scroll or to examine it. [5]One of the elders said to me, "Do not weep. The lion of the tribe of Judah, the root of David, has triumphed, enabling him to open the scroll with its seven seals."

[6]Then I saw standing in the midst of the throne and the four living creatures and the elders, a Lamb that seemed to have been slain. He had seven horns and seven eyes; these are the [seven] spirits of God sent out into the whole world. [7]He came and received the scroll from the right hand of the one who sat on the throne. [8]When he took it, the four living creatures and the twenty-four elders fell down before the Lamb. Each of the elders held a harp and gold bowls filled with incense, which are the prayers of the holy ones. [9]They sang a new hymn:

"Worthy are you to receive the scroll
and to break open its seals,
for you were slain and with your blood
you purchased for God
those from every tribe and tongue, people
and nation.

continue

extreme pain when he fears that no one is able to open the scroll and thereby dispense justice (5:4). However, when one of the elders tells him that the lion of the tribe of Judah and the root (i.e., descendant) of David will open the seals, we also learn about his qualifications to do so—he has triumphed (5:5)! The Greek word is *nikē*, meaning "to win," "to triumph," or "to win the right." But over what did he triumph?

Suddenly John sees a Lamb standing in the midst of (or as part of) the throne (5:6). This is no ordinary lamb! John says that it "seemed to have been slain" (5:6), meaning that it has the marks of having been slaughtered, but it is, in fact, alive! John observes that the Lamb has seven horns and seven eyes. Horns were thought to contain the power of an animal or an object: in this case the Lamb possesses the fullness of power (5:6). It also has seven eyes, symbolizing full knowledge or insight (5:6). Ancient people thought that an individual was able to see, not because of the light that came into the eye, but because of light that was *inside* the person. These eyes, John says, are the seven spirits of God. They are sent out into the world, bringing knowledge of all that is happening on earth (5:6).

When the Lamb steps up to receive the scroll (5:7), the four living creatures and the elders reveal in song how the Lamb won the right to open the scroll (5:8). Three actions are attributed to him: (1) he was slaughtered (i.e., crucified); (2) he ransomed the holy ones (i.e., the Christian believers); (3) he made them a kingdom and priests for God (5:9-10). Now he stands before God's throne, ready to dispense justice on God's behalf by vindicating the holy ones: they may be oppressed now, but they will reign on earth (5:10). God's holy ones are not present in heaven, but their prayers are represented before God by the four living creatures and the elders (5:8).

The scene concludes with everyone in the heavenly throne room singing in praise of the Lamb and the One seated on the throne (5:11-12). The heavenly choir numbers not in the thousands but *thousands* of thousands, suggesting a number too great to count. Everyone in the heavenly realm participates in this divine liturgy, creating a scene of perfect harmony, with no hint of suffering, pain, injustice, or evil. Finally, as if to crown this glorious moment, John observes that all created beings—those in heaven, on earth, and under the earth—join in the cosmic song of praise to God and the Lamb (5:13). The four living creatures confirm the event by saying, "Amen," meaning "So be it," and the elders worship their king (5:14).

THE SEVEN SEALS

Rev 6:1–7:17

The contents of the scroll, which the Lamb received in the previous vision, cannot be revealed until all of its seals are broken. Thus the cycle of the seven seals is closely connected to the vision of God's throne and the Lamb. Scrolls sent by kings or important dignitaries carried the seal of the sender to verify their authenticity. The seal also ensured that only the intended recipient would have access to the contents of the scroll. The four living creatures are the ones to announce the opening of the first four seals (6:1, 3, 5, 7). As each seal is broken, John receives yet another revelation. Although his vantage point for these visions is in the heavenly realm, all the activity associated with the opening of the seals takes place on earth.

6:2-8 The first four seal visions

The first four visions associated with the opening of the seals come in rapid succession. The first, the rider on the white horse, represents victory in war (6:2). Several scholars of the book of Revelation suggest that John has in mind the Parthians, whose equestrian armies were known for their skill with the bow and

The four horsemen of the apocalypse (Rev 6)

10You made them a kingdom and priests for
  our God,
    and they will reign on earth."

11I looked again and heard the voices of many angels who surrounded the throne and the living creatures and the elders. They were countless in number, 12and they cried out in a loud voice:

"Worthy is the Lamb that was slain
  to receive power and riches, wisdom and
    strength,
  honor and glory and blessing."

13Then I heard every creature in heaven and on earth and under the earth and in the sea, everything in the universe, cry out:

"To the one who sits on the throne and to
  the Lamb
    be blessing and honor, glory and might,
    forever and ever."

14The four living creatures answered, "Amen," and the elders fell down and worshiped.

IV: The Seven Seals, Trumpets, and Plagues, with Interludes

CHAPTER 6

The First Six Seals

1Then I watched while the Lamb broke open the first of the seven seals, and I heard one of the four living creatures cry out in a voice like thunder, "Come forward." 2I looked, and there was a white horse, and its rider had a bow. He was given a crown, and he rode forth victorious to further his victories.

3When he broke open the second seal, I heard the second living creature cry out, "Come forward." 4Another horse came out, a red one. Its rider was given power to take peace away from the earth, so that people would slaughter one another. And he was given a huge sword.

5When he broke open the third seal, I heard the third living creature cry out, "Come forward."

continue

I looked, and there was a black horse, and its rider held a scale in his hand. ⁶I heard what seemed to be a voice in the midst of the four living creatures. It said, "A ration of wheat costs a day's pay, and three rations of barley cost a day's pay. But do not damage the olive oil or the wine."

⁷When he broke open the fourth seal, I heard the voice of the fourth living creature cry out, "Come forward." ⁸I looked, and there was a pale green horse. Its rider was named Death, and Hades accompanied him. They were given authority over a quarter of the earth, to kill with sword, famine, and plague, and by means of the beasts of the earth.

⁹When he broke open the fifth seal, I saw underneath the altar the souls of those who had been slaughtered because of the witness they bore to the word of God. ¹⁰They cried out in a loud voice, "How long will it be, holy and true master, before you sit in judgment and avenge our blood on the inhabitants of the earth?" ¹¹Each of them was given a white robe, and they were told to be patient a little while longer until the number was

continue

who were long-standing enemies of the Romans. John observes that he *was given* a crown (6:2). The passive verb form does not reveal the giver, but John's audience would have understood it to be God. That is, God allowed the war and God handed over the defeat of the Romans to the Parthians. However, we should not understand this to mean that God is responsible for evil. Rather, John is saying that nothing happens that is outside God's control; God is sovereign in all things!

The second horse, bright red, represents bloodshed (6:4). Its rider wields his sword *by permission* (6:4), suggesting again that God is firmly in control of these earthly events. The rider takes peace from the earth, in this case, Rome, and makes people slaughter one another (6:4), a reference to the civil strife that often follows war.

When the third seal is opened and the black horse appears, John observes that its rider carries a scale for buying and selling (6:5), thus revealing another consequence of war, namely, famine. Food shortages that require someone to pay a day's wages for a day's worth of bread are extreme, to be sure. The words that announce this famine come from the midst of the four living creatures (6:6), perhaps from God or the Lamb, suggesting that God is permitting the famine or at least knows of it. The command not to damage the oil and the wine (6:6) may simply mean that God will not allow this famine to end in total annihilation. However, some scholars have suggested that oil and wine were not principally food but objects for religious ritual, and were excluded from the famine for that reason.

The opening of the fourth seal brings another horse, sickly green, the color of death (6:7-8). Its rider and Hades, the place of the dead, are given power by God to unleash all the consequences of war—killing by sword, famine, pestilence, and wild animals—on one-fourth of the earth, suggesting that their effects are comprehensive and yet limited (6:8).

John may have borrowed his imagery of four horses and their horsemen from the book of Zechariah. The prophet describes a vision of four horsemen sent by God to patrol the earth, that is, the nations that were complacent while Jerusalem suffered (Zech 1:8-17). At this point an angel appears and asks God how long Jerusalem must wait for God's mercy (Zech 1:12). The question is one of theodicy. The angel tells Zechariah to prophesy, declaring to the people that God is moved to compassion for Jerusalem and angry at the nations that did not come to its aid. The point of the prophecy of Zechariah is this: God is sovereign, but also just and merciful. So, too, in the book of Revelation: the horsemen are sent out, under God's authority, to take away the peace of Rome. In the next vision, the opening of the fifth seal, the faithful will ask how long it will be before God avenges their suffering. As he watches these visions unfold, one can imagine John being quietly gleeful, since, as we discover later, he perceives Rome to be the ultimate foe of the believing community.

6:9-11 The fifth seal vision

With the opening of the fifth seal, the scene shifts to the faithful martyrs residing under God's altar in the heavenly realm (6:9). The martyrs praise God's sovereignty and at the same time ask when God's justice will be manifest on their behalf (6:10). In response, they are given white robes, signifying victory, and told to enjoy their rest until the full number of martyrs has been reached (6:11). This is not to say that God is responsible for the martyrs' deaths, but rather that their deaths are somehow part of God's larger plan in the battle of good over evil.

6:12-16 The sixth seal vision

The opening of the sixth seal is accompanied by cosmic signs that are typical of apocalyptic literature: an earthquake, the sun turning black and the moon turning to blood, stars dropping from the heavens, and mountains falling down (6:12-14). Thus the action has shifted again to the earthly realm, though it appears that John is still in the heavens. John tells us that people of *every* social status responded to the cosmic signs with fright, begging for the earth to swallow them to protect them from God's wrath and the wrath of the Lamb (6:15-16). His point, of course, is that no one was unaffected by these phenomena. However, the intense cosmic activity (6:12-14) also suggests that all of creation is working on *God's* behalf, not theirs.

John also observes that these people are trying to avoid the *wrath* of the Lamb (6:16). A wrathful lamb is a strange paradox, because we tend to think of lambs as cute and cuddly, but already we know that it is no ordinary lamb, since earlier it was identified as the lion of the tribe of Judah and the root of David (5:5) and described as having seven horns and seven eyes (5:6). This sixth vision ends with the peoples exclaiming, "Who can withstand it?" (6:17), because it appears that *no one* will escape God's wrath.

filled of their fellow servants and brothers who were going to be killed as they had been.

[12]Then I watched while he broke open the sixth seal, and there was a great earthquake; the sun turned as black as dark sackcloth and the whole moon became like blood. [13]The stars in the sky fell to the earth like unripe figs shaken loose from the tree in a strong wind. [14]Then the sky was divided like a torn scroll curling up, and every mountain and island was moved from its place. [15]The kings of the earth, the nobles, the military officers, the rich, the powerful, and every slave and free person hid themselves in caves and among mountain crags. [16]They cried out to the mountains and the rocks, "Fall on us and hide us from the face of the one who sits on the throne and from the wrath of the Lamb, [17]because the great day of their wrath has come and who can withstand it?"

CHAPTER 7

The 144,000 Sealed

[1]After this I saw four angels standing at the four corners of the earth, holding back the four winds of the earth so that no wind could blow on land or sea or against any tree. [2]Then I saw another angel come up from the East, holding the seal of the living God. He cried out in a loud voice to the four angels who were given power to damage the land and the sea, [3]"Do not damage the land or the

continue

7:1-17 Interlude between the sixth and seventh seal visions

The situation seems dire, but there is reason for hope. In a two-part interlude between the sixth and seventh seal visions—7:1-8 and 9-17—John witnesses God's protective action on behalf of the tribes of Israel, which represent the believing community. Like the previous vision, the setting is the earthly realm. First, John sees four angels holding back the forces of destruction, perhaps another reference to the four sea or the trees until we put the seal on the foreheads of the servants of our God." ⁴I heard the number of those who had been marked with the seal, one hundred and forty-four thousand marked from every tribe of the Israelites: ⁵twelve thousand were marked from the tribe of Judah, twelve thousand from the tribe of Reuben, twelve thousand from the tribe of Gad, ⁶twelve thousand from the tribe of Asher, twelve thousand from the tribe of Naphtali, twelve thousand from the tribe of Manasseh, ⁷twelve thousand from the tribe of Simeon, twelve thousand from the tribe of Levi, twelve thousand from the tribe of Issachar, ⁸twelve thousand from the tribe of Zebulun, twelve thousand from the tribe of Joseph, and twelve thousand were marked from the tribe of Benjamin.

Triumph of the Elect

⁹After this I had a vision of a great multitude, which no one could count, from every nation, race, people, and tongue. They stood before the throne and before the Lamb, wearing white robes and holding palm branches in their hands. ¹⁰They cried out in a loud voice:

"Salvation comes from our God, who is
seated on the throne,
and from the Lamb."

¹¹All the angels stood around the throne and around the elders and the four living creatures. They prostrated themselves before the throne, worshiped God, ¹²and exclaimed:

"Amen. Blessing and glory, wisdom and
thanksgiving,
honor, power, and might
be to our God forever and ever. Amen."

¹³Then one of the elders spoke up and said to me, "Who are these wearing white robes, and where did they come from?" ¹⁴I said to him, "My lord, you are the one who knows." He said to me, "These are the ones who have survived the time of great distress; they have washed their robes and made them white in the blood of the Lamb.

continue

horsemen, so that they can do no harm to the universe (7:1; see 6:1-8). When the announcing angel orders them to hold back the forces of destruction a little longer, it becomes clear that this process of marking the servants of God with a seal (7:2-3) is for their protection. In the Greco-Roman world, people branded slaves on the forehead to indicate ownership. Likewise, in Ezekiel 9:3-4 the Lord tells Ezekiel to put a mark on the forehead of the people who grieve over the terrible things that were happening in Jerusalem. Thus the sealing of the servants of God sets them apart as belonging to God and, therefore, under God's protection. The number sealed—144,000, or 12,000 from each tribe—should be understood symbolically: perfection or fullness (12) multiplied by fullness (12), multiplied again by a number too great to count (1,000). In other words, John is not witnessing the sealing of a relatively small gathering of the elect, but an unbelievably massive crowd of people, a sea of humanity!

The second part of this interlude (7:9-17) is introduced by John's observation of a great multitude standing before the throne of God and the Lamb (7:9). The crowd that John sees is most likely the 144,000 who were sealed in the preceding scene (see 7:1-8). They are wearing robes of victory and crying out in praise and thanksgiving for the source of their salvation, namely, God and the Lamb (7:9-10). Their palm branches are symbols of victory in war (cf. 1 Macc 13:51; 2 Macc 10:7) but are also reminiscent of the feast of Tabernacles, when Jews gathered in Jerusalem to celebrate the harvest festival and build booths or tents in remembrance of God's loving care during the Exodus. This feast also anticipates the messianic age, when God's kingdom will be fully manifest and everyone will come to Jerusalem to worship God, and the whole city will be as holy as the temple (see Zech 14:16-21). In the concluding vision of the book of Revelation, the New Jerusalem (21:1–22:5), John will provide us with a fuller version of this Tabernacles motif.

Again John is permitted to witness the heavenly liturgy, with all the angels surrounding the throne, the four living creatures, the elders, and now the crowd too big to count gathering to worship God in song (7:11-12; see 5:9-14). It should be noted that their prayer contains exactly seven words of honor, symbolizing the fullness of praise to God (7:12).

Almost as if interrupting the liturgy, one of the elders asks John the identity of the ones in white robes. John defers to the elder, who then provides interpretation for him: these are the ones who have come through the persecution as martyrs, joining their blood with Christ's (7:13-14). What follows is a prophecy of consolation: they will no longer need to build tabernacles (tents) for themselves because *God* will tabernacle (i.e., shelter) them (7:15). Echoing the prophet Isaiah, the elder further declares that the white-robed crowd will never again suffer hunger, thirst, heat, or grief and, instead, will be led to springs of life-giving water (7:15-17; see Isa 49:10; 25:8).

The number **seven** is of great symbolic significance in Revelation. Some suggest it may be a key to the structure of the entire book. In Hebraic thought, seven is the perfect number; it represents wholeness and completeness. The chief opponent of the number seven is the number six, since it always falls short of perfection. Therefore 666 (Rev 13:18) is the symbolic identity of the beast.

Seven . . .	Reference
Letters	1:4–3:22
Churches	1:4–3:22
Spirits before the throne	1:4
Gold lampstands (= churches)	1:12, 20
Stars (= angels)	1:16, 20
Flaming torches (= spirits)	4:5
Seals on scroll	5:1-5
Horns and eyes on the slain Lamb (= spirits)	5:6
Trumpets	8:2–11:19
Thunders (= God's voice)	10:3
Seven thousand killed in the earthquake	11:13
Heads on the red dragon (= hills, as in Rome)	12:3; 17:9-11
Diadems on the heads of the red dragon (= kings, as in Roman emperors)	12:3; 17:9-11
Heads on the sea beast	13:1
Last plagues (cf. Exod 7–10)	15:1–16:21
Gold bowls (filled with the fury of God)	15:7; 16:1
Scenes of God's victory over evil (return of Christ; last battle; binding of Satan; thousand-year reign; defeat of Gog and Magog; last judgment; new Jerusalem)	19:11-16, 17-21; 20:1-3, 4-6, 7-10, 11-15; 21:1–22:5

> ¹⁵"For this reason they stand before God's throne
> and worship him day and night in his temple.
> The one who sits on the throne will shelter them.
> ¹⁶They will not hunger or thirst anymore,
> nor will the sun or any heat strike them.
> ¹⁷For the Lamb who is in the center of the throne will shepherd them
> and lead them to springs of life-giving water,
> and God will wipe away every tear from their eyes."

Imagine how the elder's prophecy must have sounded to John and those soon to be martyrs! It is a profoundly moving message of hope. In fact, this entire interlude (7:1-17) would have been seen as a defiantly faith-filled response to the problem of theodicy: despite appearances to the contrary, God is absolutely sovereign and just! God protects the holy ones and will surely rescue them from their sufferings, so that they can participate in this glorious liturgy of praise. John will return to these images once again in the vision of the New Jerusalem at the end of the book of Revelation (21:2–22:5).

 The **doxology** (from a Greek word meaning "prayer of praise") found in Revelation 7:12 contains ancient liturgical terms expressive of praise and gratitude (e.g., *Amen, blessing, glory*) and is read on the Solemnity of All Saints.

EXPLORING LESSON THREE

1. a) When is a vision considered to be a theophany?

_____

_____

_____

_____

_____

   b) Describe a typical Old Testament theophany (e.g., Exod 19:16-25).

_____

_____

_____

_____

_____

2. Read the prayer of the four living creatures in 4:8. How does their experience of God reflect other biblical experiences of the divine? (See Exod 3:4-5; Pss 99; 111; Isa 6:1-8; Mark 1:23-24; Luke 1:49; Heb 7:26.)

_____

_____

_____

_____

_____

3. The title "Lamb" is used to speak of Christ (5:6, 12, 13). Why is the Lamb worthy to open the scroll (5:5-10)?

_____

_____

_____

_____

_____

_____

4. How would the liturgy or prayer scene in 5:8-14 have brought comfort to John's readers?

_____

_____

_____

_____

_____

5. What powers are the four horsemen given (6:1-8), and which of these do you think represents the greatest threat to the world today? Give examples.

_____

_____

_____

_____

6. In what ways are you able to bear witness to the word of God (6:9)? What does it cost you? (See Rom 10:13-15; 2 Cor 5:20; Jas 1:19-27.)

_____

_____

_____

_____

_____

7. The souls of the faithful martyrs cry out from beneath the altar of God, asking God to "avenge [their] blood" (6:9-10). This attitude seems to be in direct conflict with teachings of Jesus regarding loving one's enemies and extending God's mercy even to those who do not seem to deserve it (see Luke 6:27-36). How do you understand this tension?

_____

_____

_____

_____

_____

8. a) What cosmic signs do we find in 6:12-14, and how do the people respond to them?

_____

_____

_____

_____

_____

b) What sign of hope can be found in these typical apocalyptic signs? (See Matt 24:29-31; Mark 13:3-8.)

_____

_____

_____

_____

_____

9. What difference does it make to be sealed as a servant of God (7:3)? (See 14:1; 2 Cor 1:21-22; Eph 1:13-14; 4:30.)

_____

_____

_____

_____

_____

_____

10. Describe the connection between forgiveness and the blood of the Lamb (7:14). (See Isa 1:18; Heb 9:22; 1 John 1:7.)

_____

_____

_____

_____

_____

_____

CLOSING PRAYER

Prayer
"For the Lamb who is in the center of the
    throne will shepherd them
and lead them to springs of life-giving water,
and God will wipe away every tear from
    their eyes."   (Rev 7:17)

Jesus, Lamb of God, we lift our voices in thanksgiving
for the gifts of grace and salvation that you have won
for us. Just as we are consoled by you, let us be a source
of consolation for others. May we always be ready to
offer relief and comfort to those in need, especially . . .

LESSON FOUR

Revelation 8–11

Begin your personal study and group discussion with a simple and sincere prayer such as:

Prayer

Heavenly Father, you are the Alpha and the Omega, our beginning and end. As we study the revelation given to your servant John, inspire us with hope in your promises and the strength to stay faithful to you always.

Read the Bible text of Revelation 8–11 found in the outside columns of pages 54–62, highlighting what stands out to you.

Read the accompanying commentary to add to your understanding.

Respond to the questions on pages 63–65, Exploring Lesson Four.

The Closing Prayer on page 66 is for your personal use and may be used at the end of group discussion.

CHAPTER 8

The Seven Trumpets

¹When he broke open the seventh seal, there was silence in heaven for about half an hour. ²And I saw that the seven angels who stood before God were given seven trumpets.

The Gold Censer

³Another angel came and stood at the altar, holding a gold censer. He was given a great quantity of incense to offer, along with the prayers of all the holy ones, on the gold altar that was before the throne. ⁴The smoke of the incense along with the prayers of the holy ones went up before God from the hand of the angel. ⁵Then the angel took the censer, filled it with burning coals from the altar, and hurled it down to the earth. There were peals of thunder, rumblings, flashes of lightning, and an earthquake.

The First Four Trumpets

⁶The seven angels who were holding the seven trumpets prepared to blow them.

⁷When the first one blew his trumpet, there came hail and fire mixed with blood, which was hurled down to the earth. A third of the land was burned up, along with a third of the trees and all green grass.

continue

THE SEVEN TRUMPETS

Rev 8:1–11:19

After the intense drama created by the opening of the previous six seals, finally the seventh and last seal is opened (8:1). The scroll could have been unrolled at this point. This is what one might have expected, especially after John's lament in Revelation 5:1-5 about finding no one worthy to open the scroll. However, surprisingly, there is no reading of its contents. Instead, there is silence in the heavens (8:1), perhaps the silence that one encounters in wor-

ship or in the presence of the divine. The rhetorical effect is to create an atmosphere of heightened anticipation. Thus the reader is forewarned that there is even greater drama to come!

 The "seven angels who stand and serve before the Glory of the Lord," traditionally known as the **angels of the presence**, are mentioned in the book of Tobit (12:15; cf. Rev 8:2), and three of them are named in the Bible: Raphael (Tob 12:15), Gabriel (Luke 1:19), and Michael (Dan 12:1; Rev 12:7). In the Jewish apocryphal scriptures, these seven angels are identified as Michael, Gabriel, Raphael, Uriel, Remiel, Sariel, and Raguel (1 Enoch 20:1-8).

Breaking the silence, John is given another vision (8:2-5), in which seven angels, probably the archangels of Jewish tradition, are given seven trumpets, a traditional symbol of the announcement of God's judgment (see Isa 27:13; Joel 2:1; Zeph 1:16). Is this the content of the scroll, revealed not in words but in visions? Perhaps, but the text does not tell us. John's vision continues when another angel is given incense with which to offer up the prayers of the believing community (8:3-4). These prayers, now rising up to God, were first voiced in Revelation 6:10—"How long will it be, holy and true master, before you sit in judgment and avenge our blood on the inhabitants of the earth?"

The angel then fills the censer with fire from the altar—God's holy fire—and throws it down to earth, where it manifests in imagery associated with apocalyptic judgment (8:5). Again the issue is theodicy. The author is asserting that nothing happens without God's permission and that God, who is sovereign, will ultimately vindicate the faithful ones.

8:6-12 The first four trumpet visions

The setting for John's visions has shifted again from the heavenly to the earthly realm (8:6), where, with the blowing of each trumpet, plagues are inflicted upon the earth. Scholars have observed that these plagues are similar in content to the plagues of the Exodus. For example, the first vision, which describes hail and fire mixed with blood being cast upon the earth, recalls the seventh plague of hail and fire in the Exodus story (8:7; see Exod 9:23-26). Likewise, the second vision describes the sea turning to blood, recalling the first plague of the Exodus story, in which the Nile River is turned to blood (8:9; see Exod 7:20). This recollection of the Exodus is interesting, especially in light of the last scene of the previous cycle of visions (7:9-17), in which the believing community and all the heavenly beings celebrate the fullness of the feast of Tabernacles, also recalling the Exodus.

The seven angels who stand closest to God's throne are the ones to announce the plagues (8:2, 7, 8, 10, 12), signaling that the plagues originate with God and descend upon the earth by God's permission. Recall that the plagues of the Exodus story were plagues only for the Egyptians; for the Hebrew peoples they were miracles, a central feature of God's liberating activity on their behalf. Likewise, by comparison, the plagues of the book of Revelation are miracles and part of God's larger plan for the salvation of the community of believers.

8When the second angel blew his trumpet, something like a large burning mountain was hurled into the sea. A third of the sea turned to blood, 9a third of the creatures living in the sea died, and a third of the ships were wrecked.

10When the third angel blew his trumpet, a large star burning like a torch fell from the sky. It fell on a third of the rivers and on the springs of water. 11The star was called "Wormwood," and a third of all the water turned to wormwood. Many people died from this water, because it was made bitter.

12When the fourth angel blew his trumpet, a third of the sun, a third of the moon, and a third of the stars were struck, so that a third of them became dark. The day lost its light for a third of the time, as did the night.

continue

This understanding of the plagues is confirmed by the scene that precedes the blowing of the trumpets: the offering of the prayers of the saints, who cry, "How long, O Lord?" (see 8:4).

Like the pattern established in the visions of the four horsemen, the first four visions of the trumpets are described very briefly and follow one another in rapid succession (8:6-13; cf. 6:1-8). However, in contrast to the visions of the four horsemen, the Roman Empire is no longer the object of destruction, but the earth itself. The destruction is substantial, and yet limited in scope, since one-third of the created world is affected by each plague (8:7, 8, 10, 11, 12). As yet, there is no mention of harm coming to the believing community or even to humanity in general. Rather, in systematic fashion, first the things of the earth are affected, then the things of the sea, followed by the things of the fresh waters, and finally the things of the heavens.

In the vision of the third trumpet, "Wormwood" is the name of the star that makes the fresh waters bitter. In the book of Jeremiah, wormwood is described as a bitter poison that God uses to punish wrongdoers (Jer 9:14; 23:15).

¹³Then I looked again and heard an eagle flying high overhead cry out in a loud voice, "Woe! Woe! Woe to the inhabitants of the earth from the rest of the trumpet blasts that the three angels are about to blow!"

CHAPTER 9

The Fifth Trumpet

¹Then the fifth angel blew his trumpet, and I saw a star that had fallen from the sky to the earth. It was given the key for the passage to the abyss. ²It opened the passage to the abyss, and smoke came up out of the passage like smoke from a huge furnace. The sun and the air were darkened by the smoke from the passage. ³Locusts came out of the smoke onto the land, and they were given the same power as scorpions of the earth. ⁴They were told not to harm the grass of the earth or any plant or any tree, but only those people who did not have the seal of God on their foreheads. ⁵They were not allowed to kill them but only to torment them for five months; the torment they inflicted was like that of a scorpion when it stings a person. ⁶During that time these people will seek death but will not find it, and they will long to die but death will escape them.

⁷The appearance of the locusts was like that of horses ready for battle. On their heads they wore what looked like crowns of gold; their faces were like human faces, ⁸and they had hair like women's hair. Their teeth were like lions' teeth, ⁹and they had chests like iron breastplates. The sound of their wings was like the sound of many horse-drawn chariots racing into battle. ¹⁰They had tails like scorpions, with stingers; with their tails they had power to harm people for five months. ¹¹They had as their king the angel of the abyss, whose name in Hebrew is Abaddon and in Greek Apollyon.

¹²The first woe has passed, but there are two more to come.

continue

8:13 Interlude between the fourth and fifth trumpet visions

In a brief interlude between the fourth and fifth trumpets (8:13), John sees and hears a bird of prey flying in the sky. The Greek word *aetos* is sometimes translated as "eagle," but "vulture" is more accurate for its connotations of impending doom. The bird cries out "Woe" three times, anticipating the three trumpets still to come, much like the prophets who cried "Woe" when they announced God's judgment against the wrongdoers. See, for example, Isaiah 3:9, 11; 45:9-10; Jeremiah 13:27; 22:13; 23:1; 48:46; Ezekiel 13:18; 16:23; 24:9.

9:1-12 The fifth trumpet vision

When the fifth trumpet is blown (9:1), we quickly learn that the woes are directed at humanity itself. The fallen star is a traditional symbol for a fallen angel or Satan (9:1; see Isa 14:12-15; Luke 10:18; Jude 13). The abyss generally refers to Sheol, the place of the dead, also called Hades. However, in Revelation it is the place where the fallen angels are imprisoned until the end-time judgment (see 17:8; 20:1-3). The key that was given to the fallen angel (9:1) is a symbol of power over the abyss, and even though God is not named, the passive form of the verb "to give" indicates that God is the giver of the key.

When the fallen angel opens the abyss, smoke pours out (9:2)—later we will see that the source of the smoke is a pool of fire within the abyss (see 20:7-10)—followed by an army of locusts (9:3). These are not ordinary locusts, because they do not eat vegetation; rather, they sting their human prey like scorpions (9:5). No one escapes their sting, except those who had been marked with the seal of God on their foreheads (9:4; see 7:1-8). In the ancient world both insects were considered offensive to humans, much as some people today feel about snakes or rats (see Luke 10:19).

John's description of the locust-scorpions—looking and sounding like horses and chariots, having crowns on their heads, and military armor where their chests should be (9:7, 9)—is reminiscent of the imagery used in the vision of the first horseman, a symbol of the Parthians (cf. 6:1-2). The "hair like women's hair" (9:8) may also refer to the Parthians, whose men were known to wear their hair long. Their reign of terror is limited to five months—half of ten—meaning a short time (9:5, 10). The name of their king, in both Hebrew and Greek, is translated as "Destruction" (9:11).

Indeed, the state of affairs looks desperate for humanity; suffering and destruction are everywhere! And yet, the careful reader will observe that God is still in control of this situation. The angel who unlocked the abyss received the key from God (9:1). The passive verb forms used to describe the activity and limitations of the locust-scorpions—"were given" (9:3), "were told" (9:4), and "were not allowed" (9:5)—all suggest that God is the all-powerful One, permitting the locusts to inflict pain and suffering. However, this is not to say that God is the cause of suffering. Rather, John is saying that evil has a *human* face (9:7), and in its destructive rampage it inflicts suffering on the whole human race. The book of Joel describes a similar plague of locusts, which God allowed for the purpose of calling people to repent (Joel 1:6-7, 15; 2:1-11; cf. Exod 10:12-15). Remember, too, that God has arranged in advance for the protection of the holy ones; they have the seal of God on their forehead (see 9:4). Thus, even in this terrible scene of destruction, John asserts that God is sovereign and just, calling people to conversion and protecting the chosen ones.

The four **"horns of the . . . altar"** (Rev 9:13) refer to the raised upper corners which Jewish altars traditionally had, in accordance with the design God commanded Moses to use when constructing the altar in Exodus 27:2.

9:13-21 The sixth trumpet vision

Immediately afterward, the sixth angel-trumpeter announces another vision: the release of the destructive forces associated with the four angels located at the four directions of

The Sixth Trumpet

[13]Then the sixth angel blew his trumpet, and I heard a voice coming from the [four] horns of the gold altar before God, [14]telling the sixth angel who held the trumpet, "Release the four angels who are bound at the banks of the great river Euphrates." [15]So the four angels were released, who were prepared for this hour, day, month, and year to kill a third of the human race. [16]The number of cavalry troops was two hundred million; I heard their number. [17]Now in my vision this is how I saw the horses and their riders. They wore red, blue, and yellow breastplates, and the horses' heads were like heads of lions, and out of their mouths came fire, smoke, and sulfur. [18]By these three plagues of fire, smoke, and sulfur that came out of their mouths a third of the human race was killed. [19]For the power of the horses is in their mouths and in their tails; for their tails are like snakes, with heads that inflict harm.

[20]The rest of the human race, who were not killed by these plagues, did not repent of the works of their hands, to give up the worship of demons and idols made from gold, silver, bronze, stone, and wood, which cannot see or hear or walk. [21]Nor did they repent of their murders, their magic potions, their unchastity, or their robberies.

continue

the universe (9:13-21). Although John does not specifically mention it, this may be the vulture's second woe (8:13; see 11:14): The order for their release comes from a voice located among the four horns of God's altar (9:13). In ancient religions the power of the deity was thought to reside in the horns of its altar. Therefore, this order comes directly from God. The fact that the angels are held ready for the exact date and time (9:15) also indicates that what is about to happen is completely under God's control. Again, the object of God's wrath is humanity, and like the previous vision, its scope is limited (one-third means a limited number; see 9:15). However, unlike the earlier vision,

CHAPTER 10

The Angel with the Small Scroll

[1]Then I saw another mighty angel come down from heaven wrapped in a cloud, with a halo around his head; his face was like the sun and his feet were like pillars of fire. [2]In his hand he held a small scroll that had been opened. He placed his right foot on the sea and his left foot on the land, [3]and then he cried out in a loud voice as a lion roars. When he cried out, the seven thunders raised their voices, too. [4]When the seven thunders had spoken, I was about to write it down; but I heard a voice from heaven say, "Seal up what the seven thunders have spoken, but do not write it down." [5]Then the angel I saw standing on the sea and on the land raised his right hand to heaven [6]and swore by the one who lives forever and ever, who created heaven and earth and sea and all that

continue

10:1–11:14 Interlude between the sixth and seventh trumpet visions

The next two visions form an interlude between the sixth and seventh trumpets, much like the interlude we saw between the opening of the sixth and seventh seals (7:1-17). The literary effect is to create a "pregnant" pause in the action, heightening the reader's anticipation for what is to come. We also have a change of setting here. In the previous six trumpet visions, John was in the heavenly realm observing what was taking place on earth. Now he is back on earth watching a mighty angel come down from heaven (10:1).

The first of these two visions (10:1-11) is reminiscent of the throne vision in Revelation 4, especially in the mention of the rainbow or halo and thunder (10:1, 3; see 4:3, 5). This angelic being also shares some features with the earlier "one like a son of man," namely, a face like the sun and legs like columns of fire (10:2; cf. 1:14-15). Apart from this angel, only two other angels in the book of Revelation are called "mighty": the angel who issued the challenge for a worthy one to come forward to

the angels are released not simply to harm their victims but to *kill* them (9:15).

Suddenly a cavalry of immense proportions appears on the scene (9:16): as a symbolic number, 200 million is double the product of ten thousand times ten thousand, which signifies fullness on top of fullness, multiplied by numbers too great to count. They come from the Euphrates River (9:14), which, in the late first-century A.D., was the eastern boundary of the Roman Empire. The horses are monstrous, with lionlike heads and serpent tails, complete with stinging mouths (9:17-19). What a nightmare! Their riders wear red, blue, and yellow armor, and the plagues they bring are fire (red), smoke (blue), and sulfur (yellow; 9:17-18). The symbolic meaning of these plagues is unclear, except that they probably represent the abyss and they kill. The purpose of the vision is revealed finally at its end. God allowed the destruction of one-third of wicked humanity in the hope that the rest would repent (9:20-21). However, they do not repent, and so we move to the next vision.

Angel with the small scroll (Rev 10)

open the scroll held by the One seated on the throne (5:2) and the angel who will throw a stone into the sea as a prophetic action against "Babylon" (18:21). Who is the mighty angel in 10:1? Most likely it is not "one like a son of man." However, it is reasonable to conclude that it is closely connected with God's glory, and that it comes with divine authority to deliver a message.

Unlike the scroll of the earlier throne vision, we are told that the scroll held by this angel is open, not closed (10:2; cf. 5:1). However, we are not told the content of the scroll. Although all the angels in the book of Revelation speak with a loud voice, this one reveals his high status through his lionlike voice and the response he receives from the seven (symbolizing fullness or perfection) thunders (10:3). When the thunders "speak" John's impulse is to write down what he hears, but he is told by another voice not to write but to "seal up" what was said (10:4). The significance of this command is unclear, except to say that humans will not be allowed access to this part of John's vision.

Many commentators interpret the **"seven thunders"** (Rev 10:3) as the voice of God. In Psalm 29, God's voice is likened to thunder and sounds seven times. There are several other instances in the Old Testament where the sound of God's voice is identified with thunder (Exod 19:19; 1 Sam 2:10; 2 Sam 22:14; Job 37:2-5). In the Gospel of John, God responds to Jesus' request ("Father, glorify your name") with a voice that many bystanders mistake for thunder (12:28-29).

Then the mighty angel raises his right hand toward heaven—the traditional position of oath-taking—and swears by the eternal One that there will be no more delay (10:5-6). He swears on God who *created heaven, earth, and sea*, thus explaining why the angel stands as he does, with one foot on the sea and the other on the land, while pointing toward the heavens.

is in them, "There shall be no more delay. [7]At the time when you hear the seventh angel blow his trumpet, the mysterious plan of God shall be fulfilled, as he promised to his servants the prophets."

[8]Then the voice that I had heard from heaven spoke to me again and said, "Go, take the scroll that lies open in the hand of the angel who is standing on the sea and on the land." [9]So I went up to the angel and told him to give me the small scroll. He said to me, "Take and swallow it. It will turn your stomach sour, but in your mouth it will taste as sweet as honey." [10]I took the small scroll from the angel's hand and swallowed it. In my mouth it was like sweet honey, but when I had eaten it, my stomach turned sour. [11]Then someone said to me, "You must prophesy again about many peoples, nations, tongues, and kings."

continue

In other words, the message he delivers pertains to the entire created order! When the seventh angel sounds his trumpet, the mystery of God will come to completion (10:7). The Greek word *mystΣrion* usually means *hidden purposes*, referring to something hidden from view.

Again John hears a heavenly voice; it is the angel who told him not to write what the seven thunders said (10:8). Now he is told to take and eat the scroll that the mighty angel is holding. The scene is reminiscent of Ezekiel, who is handed a scroll and told to eat it (Ezek 2:9–3:15). Ezekiel's scroll contains words of lament, mourning, and woe. When he first eats it, it is sweet in the mouth, but later he learns that it is directed against Israel and he goes off, in bitterness and anger, to do what God commands. For John, too, the prophecy he must deliver will at first taste sweet but in the end will bring him bitterness (10:9-10). Thus the eating of the scroll is accompanied by the command to prophesy (10:11).

Immediately John takes up his mandate, and so begins the second vision of this interlude (11:1-14). His first task is to measure the

CHAPTER 11

The Two Witnesses

¹Then I was given a measuring rod like a staff and I was told, "Come and measure the temple of God and the altar, and count those who are worshiping in it. ²But exclude the outer court of the temple; do not measure it, for it has been handed over to the Gentiles, who will trample the holy city for forty-two months. ³I will commission my two witnesses to prophesy for those twelve hundred and sixty days, wearing sackcloth." ⁴These are the two olive trees and the two lampstands that stand before the Lord of the earth. ⁵If anyone wants to harm them, fire comes out of their mouths and devours their enemies. In this way,

continue

inner parts of the Jerusalem temple, excluding the outer court of the Gentiles and those who worship there (11:1-2). The prophetic act, also seen in Ezekiel 40–43 and Zechariah 2:5-9, symbolically marks out the space where God's glory resides on earth. It also identifies the boundaries of protection for God's people.

What follows then is a message of consolation for the believers. They are told that the holy city will be overrun, but for a limited time—three and a half years, half of seven, the number representing fullness or completion (11:2). The number *three and a half* is also an allusion to Daniel 7:25 and the cruel reign of King Antiochus IV, who persecuted Jews a little more than two centuries earlier for "a year, two years, and a half-year" (NAB). In the concluding vision of the book of Revelation, the city will be measured again and established forever as the dwelling place of God and the Lamb (21:15-27).

John is now told about two unnamed witnesses (the Greek word is *martyria*), who will prophesy for forty-two lunar months, or three and a half years—the same amount of time that the city will be overrun—while wearing sackcloth, the coarse dress of prophets and a sign

of repentance (11:3). The witnesses, who are further described as two olive trees and two lamps (11:4), recall Zechariah 4–6. The two images are related, of course, because lamps were fueled by the oil from pressed olives. In the book of Zechariah the olive trees represent Zerubbabel, the anointed king of Israel and the one who laid the foundations of the temple, and Joshua, the high priest who was responsible for building the temple. These two were anointed—*messiah* means "anointed"—"who stand by the Lord of the whole earth" (Zech 4:14). Similarly, in Revelation the witnesses are said to "stand before the Lord of the earth" (11:4).

Although they are unnamed in the book of Revelation, these two witnesses appear to have connections to Elijah and Moses because of the things they are able to do to those who harm them (11:5-6). In the Old Testament stories Moses is identified with the plagues of the Exodus, especially changing water to blood (Exod 7:14-25). Elijah was said to have words like fire (Sir 48:1) and the ability to close up the heavens so that it would not rain (1 Kgs 17:1). According to the prophet Malachi, Elijah was expected to return to preach repentance before the end-time Day of Judgment (Mal 3:23-24). Deuteronomy 18:15-22 describes God's promise to raise up a prophet like Moses from among the people. Therefore the original readers of the book of Revelation would have readily recognized the connections that John was making between the witnesses in his vision and Moses and Elijah.

Without transition, the voice from heaven tells John that the witnesses, when they complete their testimony, will be attacked by the beast from the bottomless pit (11:7). We will learn more about the beast later in 13:1-8. For now, it is sufficient to say that it is the embodiment of evil. What follows is a story of the trial, unjust punishment, rescue, and vindication of the witnesses. The story follows the pattern of the Wisdom tale, which can be found throughout Jewish Wisdom literature. See, for example, the story of the vindicated righteous one in Wisdom 2:10–3:12 and some of the stories of Daniel in the book of Daniel. The Wisdom tale provides a fitting answer to the problem of the unwarranted suffering of God's holy ones, because it carries a message of consolation and hope for the persecuted: as God rescued and vindicated the righteous one in the story, so we can trust that God will rescue and vindicate us!

Here is how the Wisdom tale unfolds. As soon as the witnesses have completed their testimony, the beast conquers them and kills them (11:7). Their unburied corpses are left in the street of the "great city," probably Rome, to be viewed by passersby as a mockery and disgrace (11:8-9). The inhabitants of the earth, probably those who are in allegiance with Rome, celebrate and gloat over the destruction of the witnesses because their testimony was torment to them (11:10). Horrors! The witnesses could not have come to a worse end! But three and a half days later (symbolic of a limited time), the voice says, God comes to their rescue (11:11). God's own breath (*pneuma*, also translated "spirit") of life enters into them, and the inhabitants of the earth hear God's voice calling the witnesses, "Come up here." All the while their enemies are watching! (11:11-12). They respond with fear as they see the witnesses' restoration (11:11) because they realize the full extent of their wrongdoing, and they know that they are about to experience the full fury of God's punishment. We can almost hear their lament, "Oh, no! What did we do?" An enormous number of people (seven thousand, or a full number too great to count) fall victim to God's punishing wrath (11:13). But God's rage is also restrained—only a tenth of the population is killed. Those who remain repent and give glory to God. Thus the Wisdom tale teaches that God is sovereign and just; God will rescue the holy ones and punish the wicked. But God is also merciful and will not destroy creation forever.

A brief note on the city's symbolic names: "Sodom" and "Egypt" suggest that the city has a reputation for immorality (see Gen 18:22-32; Exod 1:11-14; and Isa 1:10). Also, the phrase "where . . . their Lord was crucified" does not refer to a place but to the forces that oppose the Christian believers (i.e., Rome; see 1 Cor 2:6-8). Parallels between the story of the two wit-

anyone wanting to harm them is sure to be slain. ⁶They have the power to close up the sky so that no rain can fall during the time of their prophesying. They also have power to turn water into blood and to afflict the earth with any plague as often as they wish.

⁷When they have finished their testimony, the beast that comes up from the abyss will wage war against them and conquer them and kill them. ⁸Their corpses will lie in the main street of the great city, which has the symbolic names "Sodom" and "Egypt," where indeed their Lord was crucified. ⁹Those from every people, tribe, tongue, and nation will gaze on their corpses for three and a half days, and they will not allow their corpses to be buried. ¹⁰The inhabitants of the earth will gloat over them and be glad and exchange gifts because these two prophets tormented the inhabitants of

continue

nesses and the story of the death and resurrection of Jesus are unavoidable and probably intentional. The reader is reminded that Jesus Christ is "*the* faithful witness" (1:5; emphasis added) of whom they are disciples.

At this point the narrator of the book of Revelation announces that the second woe has passed and the third is about to come (11:14). However, we cannot be certain which is the second woe—perhaps the releasing of the four angels at the four corners of the universe (9:13-19) or the story about the vindication of the two witnesses (11:1-13). Likewise, as we shall see, John does not clearly identify the third woe. What follows is a scene of triumph, not woe.

 The **reanimation of the two witnesses** in Revelation 11:11 recalls the means by which God breathed life into the first human at creation (Gen 2:7; Wis 15:11) and the miraculous resurrection of the dead predicted in Ezekiel's vision of the valley of the dry bones (Ezek 37:5-6).

the earth. ¹¹But after the three and a half days, a breath of life from God entered them. When they stood on their feet, great fear fell on those who saw them. ¹²Then they heard a loud voice from heaven say to them, "Come up here." So they went up to heaven in a cloud as their enemies looked on. ¹³At that moment there was a great earthquake, and a tenth of the city fell in ruins. Seven thousand people were killed during the earthquake; the rest were terrified and gave glory to the God of heaven.

¹⁴The second woe has passed, but the third is coming soon.

The Seventh Trumpet

¹⁵Then the seventh angel blew his trumpet. There were loud voices in heaven, saying, "The kingdom of the world now belongs to our Lord and to his Anointed, and he will reign forever and ever." ¹⁶The twenty-four elders who sat on their thrones before God prostrated themselves and worshiped God ¹⁷and said:

"We give thanks to you, Lord God almighty,
    who are and who were.
For you have assumed your great power
    and have established your reign.
¹⁸The nations raged,
    but your wrath has come,
    and the time for the dead to be judged,
    and to recompense your servants, the
        prophets,
    and the holy ones and those who fear
        your name,
    the small and the great alike,
    and to destroy those who destroy the earth."

¹⁹Then God's temple in heaven was opened, and the ark of his covenant could be seen in the temple. There were flashes of lightning, rumblings, and peals of thunder, an earthquake, and a violent hailstorm.

11:15-19 The seventh trumpet vision

When the seventh angel blows his trumpet (11:15), a heavenly voice announces that God's kingdom has replaced the kingdom of the world (i.e., the Roman Empire). The setting has again shifted to the heavenly realm. The twenty-four elders, who were first introduced in the throne vision of Revelation 4, fall down in worship, praising and thanking God for asserting the fullness of power against evil and rescuing the righteous believers (11:16-18). John's mention of the destroyers of the world (11:18) is probably a reference back to the king of the locust-scorpions, identified as Abaddon or Apollyon (see 9:1-12). However, it may also be a reference forward to the dragon and its two beasts that will be revealed in Revelation 12 and 13.

Suddenly the heavenly temple, even the holy of holies, is opened so that all believers can see and enjoy God's unmediated presence (11:19). The ark of the covenant, which once contained the tablets of the Sinai covenant, was lost when Solomon's temple was destroyed in 587 B.C. but is now restored in the heavenly temple (11:19). This detail recalls a legend about Jeremiah hiding the ark of the covenant and other artifacts of the temple for the day when God "gathers his people together again and shows them mercy" (2 Macc 2:7). The thunder, flashes of lightning, and other cosmic happenings (11:19) confirm that John is experiencing a theophany, that is, a manifestation of God. Thus ends the first half of the book of Revelation.

EXPLORING LESSON FOUR

1. John uses silence for dramatic effect (8:1). When has silence been especially important in your prayer life? Why?

_____

_____

_____

_____

_____

2. In Revelation 9, the situation seems desperate as plagues that disrupted the natural order are followed by plagues directed against humanity itself. Explain how the use of passive verbs (e.g., *was given, were told*) signifies hope and consolation (9:1-5).

_____

_____

_____

_____

_____

3. List attitudes, beliefs, and behaviors that may show others that you are among those who are sealed with the "seal of God" (9:4). (See Eph 1:13-14.)

_____

_____

_____

_____

4. We read that one-third of the population is destroyed, and yet the survivors still do not repent (9:18, 20-21). How can that be, and what lessons might there be here for us? (See Exod 9:12, 34; Isa 65:2; Acts 19:9.)

_____

_____

_____

_____

_____

5. John warns against worshiping idols made from gold, silver, bronze, etc. (9:20). Name some idols our culture worships, and reflect on whether there are any idols you cling to.

_____

_____

_____

_____

_____

6. Why would the command to prophesy (10:9-11) have been "sour" both to John and Ezekiel? (See Ezek 3:1-4.)

_____

_____

_____

_____

7. a) What is the connection between the two witnesses (11:3-6) and Zechariah 4–6?

_____

_____

_____

_____

  b) What other Old Testament parallel(s) could be drawn? (See Exod 7:14-24; Sir 48:1; 1 Kgs 17:1.)

_____

_____

_____

_____

8. What is the main message of the vision in 11:7-13?

_____

_____

_____

_____

_____

9. Why is the "great city" given the symbolic names of Sodom and Egypt (11:8)? (See Gen 18:22-32; Exod 1:11-14; Isa 1:10.)

_____

_____

_____

_____

_____

_____

10. a) What motivates the people to praise God in 11:13 and in 11:15-18?

_____

_____

_____

_____

_____

b) What experiences have led you to praise God?

_____

_____

_____

_____

_____

CLOSING PRAYER

Prayer

"At the time when you hear the seventh angel blow his trumpet, the mysterious plan of God shall be fulfilled, as he promised to his servants the prophets." (Rev 10:7)

Jesus, Son of God, our days are filled with uncertainty, and it is sometimes hard for us to understand the direction and meaning of our lives. May we always trust that you will guide us through all difficulties and shelter us from harm. Let us declare our confidence in you today as we pray for those who need you most, especially . . .

LESSON FIVE

Revelation 12–14

Begin your personal study and group discussion with a simple and sincere prayer such as:

Prayer

Heavenly Father, you are the Alpha and the Omega, our beginning and end. As we study the revelation given to your servant John, inspire us with hope in your promises and the strength to stay faithful to you always.

Read the Bible text of Revelation 12–14 found in the outside columns of pages 68–78, highlighting what stands out to you.

Read the accompanying commentary to add to your understanding.

Respond to the questions on pages 79–81, Exploring Lesson Five.

The Closing Prayer on page 82 is for your personal use and may be used at the end of group discussion.

CHAPTER 12

The Woman and the Dragon

¹A great sign appeared in the sky, a woman clothed with the sun, with the moon under her feet, and on her head a crown of twelve stars. ²She was with child and wailed aloud in pain as she labored to give birth. ³Then another sign appeared in the sky; it was a huge red dragon, with seven heads and ten horns, and on its heads were seven diadems. ⁴Its tail swept away a third of the stars in the sky and hurled them down to the earth. Then the dragon stood before the woman about to give birth, to devour her child when she gave birth. ⁵She gave birth to a son, a male child, destined to rule all the nations with an iron rod. Her child was caught up to God and his throne. ⁶The woman herself fled into the desert where she had a place prepared by God, that there she might be taken care of for twelve hundred and sixty days.

⁷Then war broke out in heaven; Michael and his angels battled against the dragon. The dragon and its angels fought back, ⁸but they did not prevail and there was no longer any place for them in heaven. ⁹The huge dragon, the ancient serpent, who is called the Devil and Satan, who deceived the whole world, was thrown down to earth, and its angels were thrown down with it.

¹⁰Then I heard a loud voice in heaven say:

continue

SECOND CYCLE OF VISIONS

Rev 12:1–20:15

The second half of the book of Revelation begins with an intercalation, that is, a vision inserted within another vision. This literary technique suggests that the two visions are to be interpreted together as a single, interrelated unit. The outer vision (12:1-6 and 13-17) begins in the heavens and eventually shifts to the earthly realm. Likewise, the inner vision (12:7-12) begins in the heavens and ends with a tran-

sition to earth. The outer vision (12:1-6, 13-17) describes an immense dragon attacking an unnamed woman enthroned in the heavens. The inner vision describes a war in heaven in which the angel Michael throws the dragon down to earth (12:7-12). The two visions work together to explain, in symbolic imagery, how the forces of evil came down upon God's holy ones. We will examine each vision separately, and in their parts, and then look at them together.

VISION OF THE WOMAN AND THE DRAGON

Rev 12:1-18

12:1-6 Part one of the vision of the woman and the dragon

In the opening scene of this vision, John sees an unnamed woman with the sun as her raiment, the moon as her footstool, and twelve (symbolizing fullness or perfection) stars as her crown (12:1). Without warning, the beauty and serenity of this scene are shattered by the realization that the woman is in the throes of childbirth, a traditional image for the sudden and unexpected arrival of the end time (12:2). Adding to the drama, an enormous red dragon is waiting in earnest for the child to be born so that he·can eat it as soon as it is born! (12:3-4).

In Revelation, red is the color of violence and bloodshed.

The dragon's ten horns (12:3) recall the book of Daniel, in which a ten-horned, devouring beast symbolizes the kingdom of the Greeks, who persecuted the Israelites because they refused to give up their Jewish cultural and religious practices (see Dan 7:1-28). The seven diadems or crowns (12:3) on the dragon's seven heads also signal kingship. However, the identity of the kingdom that is associated with the dragon will not be revealed until 17:1-6, where she is described as Babylon.

The message of the vision is one of consolation in the face of persecution. The woman is in a truly difficult situation, but the child born to her is male (12:5); in a patriarchal culture a male child was considered to be a sign of God's blessing. We also learn that he is destined to rule with great strength (12:5). The Greek version of Isaiah (LXX Isa 66:7) and Psalm 2:7-9 both express hope in a king who would be God's son and rule with a rod of iron.

As the vision progresses, the message of hope continues to play out in dramatic fashion. The child is rescued from the jaws of the dragon, snatched up to God (12:5), while the woman escapes to the desert, where God had made a place for her (12:6). God harbors her for a period of 1,260 days (i.e., 42 months, or three and a half years), symbolizing a limited time (12:6; see 11:3-14). Thus, although the desert is often a place of danger, here it is a place of protection.

12:7-12 Vision of the war in heaven

John leaves us wondering about the woman in the desert and now turns our attention to the inner vision (12:7-12). Immediately, the reader learns that war is about to break out in heaven (12:7). The war is quick and decisive:

Michael and his angels battle the dragon (Rev 12)

> "Now have salvation and power come,
>   and the kingdom of our God
>   and the authority of his Anointed.
> For the accuser of our brothers is cast out,
>   who accuses them before our God day
>   and night.
> [11]They conquered him by the blood of the
>   Lamb
>   and by the word of their testimony;
>   love for life did not deter them from death.
> [12]Therefore, rejoice, you heavens,
>   and you who dwell in them.
> But woe to you, earth and sea,
>   for the Devil has come down to you in
>   great fury,
>   for he knows he has but a short time."
>
> [13]When the dragon saw that it had been thrown down to the earth, it pursued the woman who had given birth to the male child. [14]But the woman was given the two wings of the great eagle, so that she could fly to her place in the desert, where, far from the serpent, she was taken care of for a year, two years, and a half-year. [15]The serpent, however, spewed a torrent of water out of his mouth after the woman to sweep her away with the current. [16]But the earth helped the woman and opened its mouth and swallowed the flood that the dragon spewed out of its mouth. [17]Then the dragon be-
>
> *continue*

the dragon and his angels are soundly defeated by the archangel Michael and his angels (12:7-8) and then tossed out of the heavenly realm (12:9)! The apocalyptic sections of the book of Daniel likewise describe the archangel Michael as a warrior prince who battles against the enemies of God's people and utterly destroys them (Dan 10:10-21; 12:1-4). Almost as a side note, we learn the dragon's names and the activity by which he is known: "the ancient serpent [referring to the snake who seduced Eve in Gen 3:1-6], who is called the Devil [literally 'slanderer' or 'enemy'] and Satan ['accuser' in Hebrew], who deceived the whole world" (12:9).

A heavenly voice confirms what John has just witnessed: the salvation, power, and sovereignty of God are now manifest (12:10a), and the accuser (i.e., prosecutor) of the woman's offspring—the persecuted believers—has been driven out of the heavens, conquered by the blood of the Lamb, Jesus Christ (12:10b-11). But the heavenly voice also warns that the dragon still needs to be driven from the other two cosmic realms, the earth and sea, and his rage will be especially intense because he knows his end is soon! (12:12).

 The church uses the poetic **prayer of praise** (Rev 12:10-12) as part of its Thursday evening prayer in the Liturgy of the Hours. It expresses the awesome power of salvation achieved in Christ.

12:13-18 Part two of the vision of the woman and the dragon

But what about the woman, whom John last saw in the desert, and how did she make her way from the heavens to the desert? The second half of the outer vision (12:13-18) provides an explanation. Unable to capture the woman's child, who was immediately taken up into heaven (12:5), the dragon is now in hot pursuit of the woman (12:13). But God rescues her, giving her two wings of an enormous bird, so that she can fly away to safety (12:14). Suddenly the great dragon becomes a huge water serpent, something like the mythical Leviathan, spewing a flood of water after her (12:15). Now God's creation comes to the woman's rescue: the earth comes alive, opening its mouth to swallow the river (12:16). Good news: the woman has escaped! One can almost imagine the dragon stomping away in fury!

At the conclusion of the vision, John observes that the dragon has turned his rage to the rest of the woman's children, the Christian believers (12:17). The reader is expected to understand, finally, the significance of the three and a half years (12:6, 14). Yes, it is the time that the woman is protected in the desert, but it is also the length of time that her children will suffer persecution. Half of seven, their persecution will be comprehensive but limited. In other words, there is reason for hope even in the midst of suffering.

But why did the author of the book of Revelation link these two visions together in this manner? Jewish tradition and Jewish apocalyptic literature in particular saw a direct connection between what was happening on earth and what was happening in the heavens. In fact, the rabbis had a saying, "As in heaven, so on earth." Thus this inner vision explains the source of the believers' persecution on earth, namely, the dragon and his angels who were thrown out of the heavenly realm, but it also promises that these evil powers will be defeated on earth just as quickly and dramatically as they were defeated in the heavens.

Given the high level of drama contained in these two visions, the reader should not be surprised that they ought to be interpreted symbolically rather than literally. We have already identified the woman's other offspring as the persecuted believers. Who, then, is the woman? John does not tell us her identity, but interpreters of the book of Revelation have advanced at least three possibilities. Some argue that the woman is Eve, because of allusions to Genesis 3:14-16, in which God curses the serpent, promising enmity between it and the woman and her offspring, and then tells the woman that her childbearing pain will intensify because of what she had done (see 12:2, 4, 9, 10).

Others argue that the woman is Mary, because the child that is snatched up to heaven is the messiah and the Lamb, by whose blood the believers are saved, that is, Jesus Christ (see 12:10-11). Still others argue that the woman represents the church, since her offspring are the persecuted believers (12:17).

The problem, of course, is that none of these identifications fit every detail of both visions. Perhaps the reader is expected to recall all three possibilities simultaneously, making these two visions a multilayered story of salvation.

Both of the visions described in Revelation 12 conclude with a reference to the dragon's fury being unleashed on earth and sea, thus

came angry with the woman and went off to wage war against the rest of her offspring, those who keep God's commandments and bear witness to Jesus. [18]It took its position on the sand of the sea.

CHAPTER 13

The First Beast

[1]Then I saw a beast come out of the sea with ten horns and seven heads; on its horns were ten diadems, and on its heads blasphemous name[s]. [2]The beast I saw was like a leopard, but it had feet like a bear's, and its mouth was like the mouth of a lion. To it the dragon gave its own power and

continue

anticipating the next two visions: the vision of the beast of the sea (13:1-10) and the vision of the beast of the land (13:11-18).

 The **symbolic woman** of Revelation 12 represents Israel of old, now renewed as a heavenly woman in the image of Eve. She is pregnant with the Messiah but must wrestle with the dragon (evil). Later Catholic tradition identified her as Mary, the mother of Jesus, because of her unique role in salvation history. Many artistic images of Mary portray her accordingly, crowned with stars and the moon at her feet, victoriously stepping on a dragon or serpent, the image of evil (see Gen 3:15).

THE VISION OF THE BEASTS OF THE SEA AND THE LAND

Rev 13:1-18

13:1-10 The beast of the sea

John's next vision is of a beast emerging from the sea. In the ancient world the sea was seen as hostile and chaotic. The four great beasts of the book of Daniel also came from the sea (Dan 7:1-8). In fact, many of the descriptors of throne, along with great authority. ³I saw that one of its heads seemed to have been mortally wounded, but this mortal wound was healed. Fascinated, the whole world followed after the beast. ⁴They worshiped the dragon because it gave its authority to the beast; they also worshiped the beast and said, "Who can compare with the beast or who can fight against it?"

⁵The beast was given a mouth uttering proud boasts and blasphemies, and it was given authority to act for forty-two months. ⁶It opened its mouth to utter blasphemies against God, blaspheming his name and his dwelling and those who dwell in heaven. ⁷It was also allowed to wage war against the holy ones and conquer them, and it was granted authority over every tribe, people, tongue, and nation. ⁸All the inhabitants of the earth will worship it, all whose names were not written from the foundation of the world in the book of life, which belongs to the Lamb who was slain.

⁹Whoever has ears ought to hear these words.
¹⁰Anyone destined for captivity goes into
        captivity.
Anyone destined to be slain by the sword
        shall be slain by the sword.

Such is the faithful endurance of the holy ones.

continue

Revelation's beast from the sea are similar to those associated with the four beasts in Daniel. For example, Daniel's fourth beast has ten horns, which represent ten kings of the Greek empire (Dan 7:7-8, 23-24). In Revelation the diadems on the ten horns also represent kingship.

Other aspects of Revelation's beast of the sea (13:2) appear to relate to the first three of Daniel's beasts: the body of a leopard (cf. Dan 7:6), the feet of a bear (cf. Dan 7:5), and the head of a lion (cf. Dan 7:4). In the book of Daniel these three beasts represent three of the great empires of history—the Babylonian empire (winged lion), the Median empire (bear), and the Persians (leopard). Thus, given John's

apparent familiarity with Daniel, we should conclude that Revelation's beast of the sea also symbolizes a very powerful empire. In John's historical context, this would be the Roman Empire (see also 6:1-8).

John describes the beast of the sea in considerable detail, but the details are to be understood metaphorically. Its seven heads (13:1) describe the fullness of power. The blasphemous name on its heads (13:1) probably refers to titles regularly given to the Roman emperors of John's day—"Lord," "Lord and God," and "Savior of the World"—all of which the Christian believer would have considered to be blasphemies against God. The blasphemies it utters (13:5) refer to its offenses against God and the Christians who worship God.

Regarding the detail about the beast's head seeming to have been "mortally wounded, but this mortal wound was healed" (13:3), some scholars conclude that the beast is the emperor Nero (d. A.D. 68), who committed suicide, leaving the empire in civil war for a year before Vespasian took the throne and restored the empire in A.D. 69. However, it is also likely that John is making a parody on the Lamb "that seemed to have been slain" (5:6). Thus, with much disdain, he writes that the people of the whole earth are completely enamored of the Roman Empire. They worship the Roman Empire, saying that there is no other like it and no one can stand against it, and they worship the dragon (i.e., Satan), from whom the Roman Empire gets its authority (13:3-4). But all this is so much foolishness! *God* is the one they should worship. And the Lamb, who gets its authority from God, is the one against whom no one can stand!

Worship of the dragon and the beast (13:4) is probably a reference to the emperor cult, in which people were obligated to offer sacrifices to the emperor in order to ensure the empire's prosperity. Christians who refused to participate were considered a threat to the empire. However, John reminds his readers that Rome has no power except what was given it by God. For this reason, John uses the passive forms of the verbs "to give" and "to permit." The beast, John says, "*was given* authority to act" (13:5;

emphasis added), "*was also allowed* to wage war against the holy ones" (13:7; emphasis added), and "*was granted* authority over every tribe, people, tongue, and nation" (13:7). Thus John is asserting that God is sovereign over everyone and everything, even as the Roman Empire reigns over the whole world and God's holy ones are being killed by its emperor.

The holy ones, however, should be consoled by the fact that the time of their suffering is limited: Rome can act for only three and a half years, half of seven, the number of fullness (13:5). They should also be consoled by the fact that the names of the ones who worship the beast will *not* be found in the Lamb's book of life (13:8), while theirs most surely will be, as long as they remain faithful.

Thus John concludes this vision with a prophetic admonition directed to the Christian community. He begins with a riddle (13:10) that sounds like some kind of teaching on predestination, but most scholars agree that it is not; rather, it is a call for endurance and trust, no matter what the cost. If the Christian community opposes the beast (i.e., the Roman Empire) and refuses to worship it, they should expect suffering and even death, because it is

> ### The Second Beast
>
> [11]Then I saw another beast come up out of the earth; it had two horns like a lamb's but spoke like a dragon. [12]It wielded all the authority of the first beast in its sight and made the earth and its inhabitants worship the first beast, whose mortal wound had been healed. [13]It performed great signs, even making fire come down from heaven to earth in the sight of everyone. [14]It deceived the inhabitants of the earth with the signs it was allowed to perform in the sight of the first beast,
>
> *continue*

an inevitable outcome of their opposition. However, that is not their concern. Whatever happens, their only response should be faithful perseverance (13:10).

13:11-18 The beast from the earth

Immediately following the vision of the beast from the sea, John receives a vision of a beast rising from the earth (13:11-18). Like the beast from the sea, this beast is related to the

 Revelation is essentially one long, complex vision of God's ultimate victory over evil. It is filled with **symbolic language** for the sake of the original Christian audience who lived in a time of persecution by Roman authorities. The following chart lists some of these symbols in Revelation 12–17.

Symbols	Reference
Woman adorned with the sun, the moon, and stars, most likely representing the new people of Israel (the church); Roman Catholics traditionally see in her the image of Mary.	12:1
Red dragon representing Satan, evil personified	12:3
Beast from the sea representing the Roman Empire and its emperors	13:1
Beast with the number 666, most likely representing Caesar Nero	13:18
144,000 of the elect who are ransomed, representing the twelve tribes of Israel	14:3
Babylon, symbolic of Rome	14:8; 16:19; 17:5; 18:2
The harlot, representing Babylon (Rome); Old Testament background of harlotry as idolatry (e.g., Hos 1:2; 2:4-15)	17:1-18

telling them to make an image for the beast who had been wounded by the sword and revived. [15]It was then permitted to breathe life into the beast's image, so that the beast's image could speak and [could] have anyone who did not worship it put to death. [16]It forced all the people, small and great, rich and poor, free and slave, to be given a stamped image on their right hands or their foreheads, [17]so that no one could buy or sell except one who had the stamped image of the beast's name or the number that stood for its name.

[18]Wisdom is needed here; one who understands can calculate the number of the beast, for it is a number that stands for a person. His number is six hundred and sixty-six.

continue

dragon. In fact, it *speaks* like the dragon (13:11). Further, it exercises all the authority of the first beast, which received *its* authority from the dragon (13:12). Therefore, if the first beast is the Roman Empire, then the second must be its representative, the emperor.

The narrator of John's vision makes clear that this beast is a deceiver. He has horns that make him look like a lamb, but he has the voice of the dragon, the embodiment of all that is evil (13:11). He works miracles like the prophets of Israel, even like Elijah, the prophet who could call down fire from heaven and who was expected to return in the end time (Rev 13:13-14; see 1 Kgs 18:38; 2 Kgs 1:10; and Rev 11:3-14 on the two witnesses who were prophets). In sum, he is a false prophet whose goal it is to deceive the whole world. Although John does not use the term, some scholars have called this beast the anti-Christ, because it gives the *appearance* of being the Christ ("anointed"), but clearly is not.

Again John uses the passive form of certain verbs to indicate that the beast acts with God's permission. Thus the narrator of this vision says that the beast "was allowed" to perform miracles (13:14) and give life to the image (i.e., statue) of the beast (13:15). In effect, John is saying that the deceptive activity of the beast is somehow part of God's plan. However, we should not interpret this to mean that God is the source of evil. Rather, John is asserting that God remains sovereign over all things, even over the emperor, despite appearances to the contrary.

John indicates that the stranglehold of the emperor extended beyond religion to politics and economics, since everyone was required to have the mark of the beast on their right hand and on their head (13:16). The mark on the head recalls the first-century A.D. practice of branding slaves on the forehead to show whose property they were. Thus the mark of the beast is most likely a reference to the official seal of the emperor, which was used to authenticate imperial documents and identify the emperor's property. The image of the emperor was also imprinted on all the coins of the empire, so a person could not even buy or sell without indirectly participating in the emperor cult (see 13:17). Again, the reader should not take this talk of branding literally. Rather, John intends that we treat it metaphorically and contrast this mark of the beast with the mark of the Lamb that was placed upon the forehead of God's holy ones (see 7:2-3). Either you belong to the Lamb or you belong to the beast! If you belong to the Lamb, you are protected from the catastrophes of the end time; but if you belong to the beast, you will suffer the same fate that he will suffer.

At the conclusion of this vision, John adds a note to his readers concerning the identity of the beast from the earth (13:18). To appreciate what John is saying here, we must imagine a community that already knows the identity of the beast and, together with John, shares a bit of "naughty" delight in talking about the beast behind his back! The practice in which John is engaged is called *gematria*. Jewish rabbis of the ancient world were skilled at it, but non-Jewish people in the Greco-Roman world enjoyed it too. It was a process of assigning numbers to letters of a word or a name and using the resulting number to designate something about the holder of that name.

Because Latin, Hebrew, and Greek do not have separate sets of symbols for numbers, people used the individual letters and combinations of letters to designate quantities. It became quite natural, then, to refer to a person by their number, particularly among friends who wished to share a "secret" that they wanted to keep from outsiders. People who already knew the name could very quickly discern the number, but those who did not would find it almost impossible to solve the riddle. Sometimes the number also has symbolic meaning, as in the case of 666. Six is one short of perfection or fullness and therefore means imperfection or evil. Thus John is saying to his audience, "Here is this beast who has deceived and enamored the whole world, but *we* know who he really is—he is evil itself!"

What, then, is the name of the beast? Since he appears to be one of the emperors of Rome, and presumably someone known to John, our choices have been narrowed considerably. Most scholars believe him to be Nero, since his Greek name and title, transliterated into Hebrew, adds up to 666: N(50) + r(200) + o(6)+ n(50) + Q(100) + s(60) + r(200), while his Latin name and title, transliterated into Hebrew, adds up to 616: N(50) + r(200) + o(6) + Q(100) + s(60) + r(200), which is a variant reading found in some of the manuscripts (handwritten copies) of the book of Revelation. Nero was already deceased at the time of John's writing, but because of the legend associated with his departure and because he, like Domitian after him, also persecuted Christian believers, some have concluded that Domitian was Nero returned to life.

VISION OF THE LAMB AND IMMINENT JUDGMENT

Rev 14:1-20

14:1-5 Vision of the Lamb on Mount Zion

As a counterpoint to the visions of the dragon and its two beasts, John has another vision—this time of the Lamb standing on Mount Zion, also known as Jerusalem (14:1-5). Instead of the inhabitants of the world who

---

CHAPTER 14

The Lamb's Companions

[1]Then I looked and there was the Lamb standing on Mount Zion, and with him a hundred and forty-four thousand who had his name and his Father's name written on their foreheads. [2]I heard a sound from heaven like the sound of rushing water or a loud peal of thunder. The sound I heard was like that of harpists playing their harps. [3]They were singing [what seemed to be] a new hymn before the throne, before the four living creatures and the elders. No one could learn this hymn except the hundred and forty-four thousand who

continue

---

wear the mark of the beast, John sees the 144,000—fullness upon fullness multiplied by a number too great to count—wearing the mark of the Lamb and his Father (14:1; cf. 13:16-17). These are the same 144,000 who were sealed in 7:1-8. In constructing this image, the author may have in mind Psalm 2: "I myself have installed my king / on Zion, my holy mountain" (Ps 2:6). In traditional Judaism this is the place where the remnant of Israel would be gathered together in the messianic age (Joel 3:5; Obad 17; Mic 4:6-8; Zeph 3:12-20).

As the vision proceeds, John hears sounds—something like rushing water, thunder, and harps (14:2)—that are usually associated with theophany (i.e., manifestation of God; cf. 1:15; 5:8; 15:2; 19:6). Further, the mention of the throne, the elders, and four living creatures (14:3) recalls the throne vision of Revelation 4, suggesting some direct connection between Zion (Jerusalem) and the heavenly throne room. Again, in contrast to the multitudes who worship the beast in the preceding vision (13:8), John sees the 144,000 singing a "new hymn" in praise of God and the Lamb (14:3). The "new hymn" is probably the same one sung by the heavenly court in 5:8-10. In it the heavenly host praised the Lamb, who is deemed worthy to had been ransomed from the earth. ⁴These are they who were not defiled with women; they are virgins and these are the ones who follow the Lamb wherever he goes. They have been ransomed as the firstfruits of the human race for God and the Lamb. ⁵On their lips no deceit has been found; they are unblemished.

The Three Angels

⁶Then I saw another angel flying high overhead, with everlasting good news to announce to those who dwell on earth, to every nation, tribe, tongue, and people. ⁷He said in a loud voice, "Fear God and give him glory, for his time has come to sit in judgment. Worship him who made heaven and earth and sea and springs of water." ⁸A second angel followed, saying:

"Fallen, fallen is Babylon the great,
    that made all the nations drink
    the wine of her licentious passion."

⁹A third angel followed them and said in a loud voice, "Anyone who worships the beast or its image, or accepts its mark on forehead or hand,

continue

break the seals on God's scroll because he redeemed all peoples and nations by his blood.

John observes that not everyone, but only the 144,000 who have been "ransomed from the earth" (14:3), can learn this song. They are the ones who were marked on their foreheads with the seal of God before the destructive forces were unleashed from the four corners of the world (7:3). Here, John adds, they "follow the Lamb wherever he goes" (14:4), most likely a reference to their perseverance, even to the point of suffering and death (14:3-4). Pure in every way, they are God's perfect sacrifice; they are the firstfruits, the first and best of the harvest, offered on behalf of all God's people (14:4-5). For persecuted Christians, this is the motivation for their faithful endurance: the

opportunity to participate in the true heavenly liturgy.

The significance of the detail about the 144,000 who had not defiled themselves with sexual activity (14:4) is not altogether clear. Some scholars have suggested that this vision represents the gathering of God's army in anticipation of holy war, since soldiers who engaged in holy war were expected to abstain from sexual activity during military service. Others have argued that sexual abstinence is consistent with their role as priests in this heavenly liturgy. Still others have suggested that the virginal state of the 144,000 should be viewed as a metaphor for their refusal to participate in the emperor cult, since Jewish and early Christian writings often describe idol worship in terms of prostitution and adultery. Whether one or all of these meanings are intended, we can be quite sure that it should not be taken literally, so as to say that only celibate Christians are redeemed.

The author of Revelation has already made use of **Psalm 2** several times earlier in the text (2:27; 11:18; 12:5). By associating the Lamb with the king who stands on Mount Zion (the mountain upon which Jerusalem, the capital of Judah, was built; see Ps 2:6), Revelation 14:1 emphasizes the association between the Lamb and the Lion of Judah already drawn in Revelation 5:5-6. The militant pose of the Lamb standing on top of a mountain also suggests its superiority to the dragon, which takes "its position on the sand of the sea" (12:18).

14:6-20 Visions of imminent judgment

Three more "mini" visions, or perhaps extensions of the previous vision, now follow in rapid succession (14:6-13, 14-16, 17-20). Together they represent the "good news" of God's coming judgment.

The first of these visions is introduced with the phrase "I saw another angel" (14:6), which will be repeated two more times before its end, as a second and third angel appear. The first angel flies into the midheaven announcing (literally, "evangelizing") an eternal gospel (literally, "good news"; the Greek word is *euangelion*) for all people (14:6). It is a call to repentance and an invitation to worship the one true God, who made the heavens, the earth, and the sea—the place from which the dragon was thrown down and the places where the beast of the earth and the beast of the sea currently reside, though not for long! The good news is that the time for God's judgment has come (14:7). The reader will recall that the great-winged vulture, who announced the three woes, also flew in the midheaven (see 8:13). It was understood to be the place that stretched across the entire created world.

A second angel appears with a prophetic message of doom for Babylon: the "great" city that made its peoples drunk on its enticements and practices of idol worship has fallen! (14:8). In 1 Peter 5:13 Rome is referred to as "Babylon," and there is every reason to suppose the same meaning is intended here.

The third angel appears with an admonition: whoever gives in to the enticements of the Roman Empire and participates in its cultic practices will also experience the full force of the wrath of God (14:9-10). Of whom is he speaking? Fellow Christians? This is certainly possible! One can probably imagine a situation in which a person decides to keep quiet and go along with the crowd rather than risk persecution or death. For this reason, John again calls his hearers to faithful endurance (14:12) by warning them what is in store if they fail in their perseverance (14:10-11). A heavenly voice adds authority to John's admonition with a beatitude: "Blessed are the dead who die in the Lord" (14:13). The Spirit confirms it with a second blessing: the dead will be able to rest, knowing that their deeds (i.e., their witness to the faith) will follow them after death (14:13).

In the next vision John sees "one who looked like a son of man" seated on a white cloud (14:14). The crown on his head represents kingship. The sickle, necessary equipment for

---

^{10}will also drink the wine of God's fury, poured full strength into the cup of his wrath, and will be tormented in burning sulfur before the holy angels and before the Lamb. ^{11}The smoke of the fire that torments them will rise forever and ever, and there will be no relief day or night for those who worship the beast or its image or accept the mark of its name." ^{12}Here is what sustains the holy ones who keep God's commandments and their faith in Jesus.

^{13}I heard a voice from heaven say, "Write this: Blessed are the dead who die in the Lord from now on." "Yes," said the Spirit, "let them find rest from their labors, for their works accompany them."

The Harvest of the Earth

^{14}Then I looked and there was a white cloud, and sitting on the cloud one who looked like a son of man, with a gold crown on his head and a sharp sickle in his hand. ^{15}Another angel came out of the temple, crying out in a loud voice to the one sitting on the cloud, "Use your sickle and reap the harvest, for the time to reap has come, because the earth's harvest is fully ripe." ^{16}So the one who was sitting on the cloud swung his sickle over the earth, and the earth was harvested.

continue

---

harvesting grain, is also a traditional symbol of God's judgment (see Isa 17:5; 27:12; Jer 51:33; Joel 3:13). The color white signals victory (14:14). Although the "one who looked like a son of man" is unnamed, we may safely conclude that he is Jesus Christ, because of the initial vision, in which he is revealed to be the risen Jesus (1:13). The imagery is borrowed from Daniel 7:9-14, a vision in which "one like a son of man" comes on the clouds and is presented before the "Ancient One" and given dominion over all nations and peoples. His will be an everlasting kingdom, in contrast to the kingdom of the fourth beast, who made war on the "holy ones" of God and reigned with terrifying strength, but only until the Ancient

> ¹⁷Then another angel came out of the temple in heaven who also had a sharp sickle. ¹⁸Then another angel [came] from the altar, [who] was in charge of the fire, and cried out in a loud voice to the one who had the sharp sickle, "Use your sharp sickle and cut the clusters from the earth's vines, for its grapes are ripe." ¹⁹So the angel swung his sickle over the earth and cut the earth's vintage. He threw it into the great wine press of God's fury. ²⁰The wine press was trodden outside the city and blood poured out of the wine press to the height of a horse's bridle for two hundred miles.

One arrived and pronounced judgment in favor of the "holy ones." In Daniel the fourth beast is the Greek empire and its king, Antiochus IV, who was notorious for his persecution of the Jewish people.

One can easily imagine John juxtaposing his own "one like a son of man," a heavenly warrior and deliverer of justice, against Rome and its emperor, represented by the great dragon and its beasts. In John's vision "one like a son of man" waits, poised for the harvest, until he hears the angel's command to begin the reaping (14:14-16). On first view, it might seem strange that Jesus Christ has to wait for the angel's command, but the angel is merely God's messenger (the Greek word *angelos* means "messenger"). It is God who is in charge! This harvest appears to refer to the gathering in of all humanity, because no distinction is made between righteous and wicked.

Another vision, also of judgment, follows immediately (14:17-20). In it John sees another angel wielding a sickle (14:17). The angel's job is to harvest the grapes of the earth, and his orders came from the angel in charge of the fire of the altar (14:18). The angel at the altar is the one who earlier offered up the prayers of the

"holy ones" and then filled the censer with fire and threw it on the earth (8:3-5). Recall, also, that the souls of the martyrs have been resting under the altar, waiting for the day when God will vindicate them (6:9-10). Thus this vision is another response to the question raised by the martyred souls: "How long will it be . . . before you sit in judgment and avenge our blood on the inhabitants of the earth?" (6:10). They need not wait any longer because the time of judgment has come!

The angel's activity of harvesting the grapes and throwing them into the "great wine press of God's fury" (14:19) is a traditional metaphor for judgment. See, for example, Isaiah 63:1-6, Joel 4:13, and Jeremiah 25:30. Although the narrator of the vision does not make it explicit, this judgment imagery is double-edged. For the owners and recipients of the fruits of the vineyard, harvest and winemaking are joyous events. But there can be no wine without first smashing the grapes and extracting their blood (i.e., juice). Therefore this harvest also involves suffering and pain.

John observes that God's wrath is so furious and God's judgment so comprehensive that the "blood" runs like a river, as deep as a horse's bridle and as far as two hundred miles (literally, 1,600 *stadia*; 14:20). Again, for the owner of the vineyard this is an astounding amount of wine, indicative of intensive and long-lasting joy! The Greek *stadion* (singular) measures about 606 feet, so 1,600 *stadia* total approximately 183 miles. More important, however, are the symbolic meanings of this number. It is 40 multiplied by 40, with 40 symbolizing a period of transition or transformation. It is also 4 multiplied by 4 multiplied by 10 multiplied by 10, with 4 being the universal number and 10 representing fullness or completion. In other words, this judgment is wholly transformative and/or fully comprehensive, and God's power over evil is absolute.

EXPLORING LESSON FIVE

1. Identify three symbols or messages of hope and consolation in the vision of the woman and the dragon (12:1-6).

_____

_____

_____

_____

_____

_____

2. a) What does the battle between Michael and the dragon symbolize (12:7-9)? (See Col 1:13.)

_____

_____

_____

_____

_____

   b) Do you find "battle" imagery to be a helpful way of envisioning the tension between good and evil? Or do you find it problematic? Reflect on the benefits and the difficulties of this biblical language.

_____

_____

_____

_____

3. Identify the dragon's names (12:9) and discuss whether they are fitting names for evil. (See Gen 3:12-16.)

_____

_____

_____

_____

_____

_____

4. "Fascinated, the whole world followed after the beast" (13:3). What "fascinations" distract you from your commitment to Christ, especially to prayer and service? (See Col 2:8.) How have you been successful in resisting these distractions?

_____

_____

_____

_____

_____

_____

5. John uses coded language to describe common Roman practices and demands made of Roman citizens. What are these practices and demands (13:11-17)? (See 19:20; Matt 24:24.)

_____

_____

_____

_____

_____

_____

6. What does the number 666 most likely symbolize (13:18), and in what ways have you heard this Scripture verse misused?

_____

_____

_____

_____

_____

_____

7. Why is Babylon associated with God's judgment (14:8)? (See 18:1-24; Isa 21:9; Jer 51.)

_____

_____

_____

_____

_____

_____

8. Read the vision in 14:9-13. What symbolic imagery in this vision would have encouraged those who were loyal to God's covenant to persevere? What would have encouraged the disloyal to repent?

_____

_____

_____

_____

_____

_____

9. How do you reconcile the picture of God's fury in 14:10-11 with more gentle and protecting images found elsewhere in the Bible? (See Ps 23; Isa 40:11; Hosea 11:1-4; Matt 11:28-30; Luke 13:34; John 11:33-36.)

_____

_____

_____

_____

_____

_____

10. Revelation 12–14 contains many striking, unusual images. Which one in particular spoke to your imagination? Why?

_____

_____

_____

_____

_____

_____

CLOSING PRAYER

Prayer

Whoever has ears ought to hear these words. (Rev 13:9)

Lord Jesus Christ, Word of God, wake our slumbering minds and hearts, and open our ears when we listen to your word but do not truly hear it. Help us to be aware of your voice as you speak to us in Scripture, in the world you created, and through the people you inspire. Today may we prove our willingness to serve you, especially by . . .

LESSON SIX

Revelation 15–18

Begin your personal study and group discussion with a simple and sincere prayer such as:

Prayer

Heavenly Father, you are the Alpha and the Omega, our beginning and end. As we study the revelation given to your servant John, inspire us with hope in your promises and the strength to stay faithful to you always.

Read the Bible text of Revelation 15–18 found in the outside columns of pages 84–93, highlighting what stands out to you.

Read the accompanying commentary to add to your understanding.

Respond to the questions on pages 94–96, Exploring Lesson Six.

The Closing Prayer on page 97 is for your personal use and may be used at the end of group discussion.

CHAPTER 15

The Seven Last Plagues

¹Then I saw in heaven another sign, great and awe-inspiring: seven angels with the seven last plagues, for through them God's fury is accomplished.

²Then I saw something like a sea of glass mingled with fire. On the sea of glass were standing those who had won the victory over the beast and its image and the number that signified its name. They were holding God's harps, ³and they sang the song of Moses, the servant of God, and the song of the Lamb:

"Great and wonderful are your works,
 Lord God almighty.
Just and true are your ways,
 O king of the nations.
⁴Who will not fear you, Lord,
 or glorify your name?
For you alone are holy.
 All the nations will come
 and worship before you,
 for your righteous acts have been revealed."

continue

VISIONS OF THE SEVEN BOWLS

Rev 15:1–16:21

John signals a transition to a new and important series of visions with the phrase "Then I saw in heaven another sign, great and awe-inspiring" (15:1). Elsewhere the word "sign" is used only of the woman enthroned in the heavens (12:1) and the great dragon (12:3). This third series of seven visions—the first was the opening of the seals (6:1–7:17), and the second the visions of the trumpets (8:1–9:19)—will be the last because, the reader is told, God's wrath is coming to completion in them (15:1).

15:2-8 Another vision of heavenly liturgy

Before these seven bowls of the seven plagues are unleashed, John is privileged to witness again the heavenly liturgy. The floor that looks like a sea of glass (15:2) is reminiscent of the throne vision in Revelation 4. The fact that it is mingled with fire (15:2) may indicate that God's judgment is about to be rendered, or it may signal that only those tried by fire—the persecuted—may enter. The latter view is supported by John's observation that the singers who hold God's harps are the ones who endured faithfully against the wicked enticements of the dragon and his two beasts (15:2-3). They were earlier identified as the 144,000 who were sealed with the name of God on their forehead (7:1-8; 14:1-5).

The "song of Moses" (15:3) is an allusion to Exodus 15:1-18, the song that Moses and the Israelites sang in praise of God, who rescued them by unleashing the plagues on the Egyptians. John's version of the song is made up of phrases from throughout the Old Testament (Rev 15:3-4; see Ps 111:2; 139:14; Amos 4:13; Ps 145:17; Deut 32:4; Jer 10:7; Ps 86:9; Mal 1:11; Ps 98:2), making it a song in praise of God's justice and sovereignty. It also proclaims the goal of God's mighty deeds: that all God's peoples come together in worship.

The preparations for the release of the seven plagues are now underway. John sees the opening of the tent of witness, an allusion to the tent of meeting of the Exodus (15:5; see

Exod 33:7-11). The seven angels who emerge (15:6) are wearing golden sashes, reminiscent of the priests of the temple, but also like the "one like a son of man" in Revelation's initial vision (see 1:6). Their white linen robes are a symbol of victory (see also 19:8, 14). They come out of the temple with seven plagues and then receive the implements of judgment—the bowls of the wrath of God—from one of the four living creatures who stand before the altar of God. The point of the vision is this: God is the source of these plagues. The smoke in the temple (15:8) suggests that God now inhabits it and will remain there until the seven angels complete their assigned task. This is why no one can enter the temple until the plagues are finished (15:9).

16:1-9 The first four bowl visions

The "loud voice" (16:1) that speaks from the temple, issuing the order to pour out the plagues, presumably is God's (see 15:8). Like the first four visions of the seals series (6:1-8) and the trumpets series (8:6-12), the pouring out of the first four bowls comes in rapid succession. Further, like the trumpets series, these visions recall the plagues of the Exodus. Thus the first bowl is poured out on earth, and people whose allegiance is with the dragon and its beasts develop boils and other skin diseases (16:2; see Exod 9:10-11). The second is poured into the sea, the sea turns to blood, and everything in it dies (16:3). The third is poured into the rivers and fresh water springs, and they, too, turn to blood (16:4-7; Exod 7:17-21).

Suddenly the angel of the waters (ancient peoples believed that there were heavenly beings in charge of the various elements of creation, like guardian angels) breaks out in a prayer in praise of God's justice (15:5). Those who killed the holy ones and prophets have received their just "reward," he says. They now have only blood to drink! (15:6). As this vision closes, the altar itself joins in the angel's prayer of praise. Of course, altars cannot talk, so the author may be using the literary technique of personification to refer to the angel of the altar or the souls of the martyrs who have been wait-

---

⁵After this I had another vision. The temple that is the heavenly tent of testimony opened, ⁶and the seven angels with the seven plagues came out of the temple. They were dressed in clean white linen, with a gold sash around their chests. ⁷One of the four living creatures gave the seven angels seven gold bowls filled with the fury of God, who lives forever and ever. ⁸Then the temple became so filled with the smoke from God's glory and might that no one could enter it until the seven plagues of the seven angels had been accomplished.

CHAPTER 16

The Seven Bowls

¹I heard a loud voice speaking from the temple to the seven angels, "Go and pour out the seven bowls of God's fury upon the earth."

²The first angel went and poured out his bowl on the earth. Festering and ugly sores broke out on those who had the mark of the beast or worshiped its image.

³The second angel poured out his bowl on the sea. The sea turned to blood like that from a corpse; every creature living in the sea died.

⁴The third angel poured out his bowl on the rivers and springs of water. These also turned to blood. ⁵Then I heard the angel in charge of the waters say:

"You are just, O Holy One,
    who are and who were,
    in passing this sentence.

continue

---

ing *under* the altar for God to avenge their deaths (6:9-11). The altar's words, "Your judgments are true and just" (16:7), would suggest that the martyrs are now satisfied that God has answered their plea.

When the fourth bowl is poured out on the sun, scorching the people of the earth, John observes that its victims cursed the name of God (16:8-9). The language is reminiscent of the beast of the sea that blasphemes against

⁶For they have shed the blood of the holy
    ones and the prophets,
    and you [have] given them blood to drink;
    it is what they deserve."

⁷Then I heard the altar cry out,

"Yes, Lord God almighty,
    your judgments are true and just."

⁸The fourth angel poured out his bowl on the sun. It was given the power to burn people with fire. ⁹People were burned by the scorching heat and blasphemed the name of God who had power over these plagues, but they did not repent or give him glory.

¹⁰The fifth angel poured out his bowl on the throne of the beast. Its kingdom was plunged into darkness, and people bit their tongues in pain ¹¹and blasphemed the God of heaven because of their pains and sores. But they did not repent of their works.

¹²The sixth angel emptied his bowl on the great river Euphrates. Its water was dried up to prepare the way for the kings of the East. ¹³I saw three unclean spirits like frogs come from the mouth of the

continue

continue

God's use of **plagues and natural disasters** in Revelation as a last-ditch effort to move sinners to repentance recalls similar attempts to compel Israel to right observance of the law in the years leading up to the destruction of Jerusalem and the temple. In Amos, for example, God recalls how famine, drought, blight, pestilence, and war were sent to convince the nation to return to faithful covenant living, but all to no avail (4:6-11). God's efforts are no more successful in Revelation (16:9, 11).

16:10-21 The last three bowl visions

The fifth bowl, which is poured upon the throne of the beast, results in darkness over its entire kingdom (16:10; cf. Exod 10:21). This is not the peaceful darkness of sleep, but a desperate darkness that drives people to great anguish, even to swearing against God, as their suffering from the earlier plagues is intensified. The narrator adds, "But they did not repent of their works" (16:11). As we shall see in Revelation 17–18, these people are the worshipers of Babylon (i.e., Rome), and their works are the activities that support the power of the beast, namely, politics, commerce, and cultic practices of the Roman Empire.

The sixth bowl is poured out in the Euphrates River, then the eastern border of the Roman Empire, and it dried up, so that armies from the East could enter the empire (16:12). John probably has in mind the Parthians, who were longtime enemies of the Romans (see also 6:1-2 and 9:14). Suddenly John sees unclean spirits emerge from the mouths of the dragon, the beast of the sea, and the beast of the land (here called "the false prophet" because of his deception, 16:13; cf. 12:3; 13:1, 11, 14). The narrator adds that they are "demonic" (that is, deceptive) spirits. John compares the demonic spirits to frogs, recalling the locust-scorpions in Revelation 9:1-9, which elicit feelings of disgust or dislike, but also suggesting the Exodus plague of frogs (Exod 7:25–8:15). The "kings of the

God (13:1, 5-6) and also anticipates the description of the whore Babylon, who rides a beast covered in blasphemies (17:3). By cursing God the people identify themselves with the dragon and the beasts that get their authority from the dragon. However, the mention of repentance also recalls Pharaoh's response to the Exodus plagues: he expresses the desire to repent until the plague is removed and then returns to his obdurate behavior. Whatever the response of the people, the goal of God's wrath is clear: to call people to repentance and to worship of the one true God. These plagues are not simply gratuitous violence on God's part, but rather a tool for conversion. But the people do not repent or give God glory (16:9).

whole world" (16:14) probably refers to the kings of the *Roman* world, as distinct from the kings of the East. As John describes it, the three unclean spirits are responsible for all the kings of the earth rallying to war; their assembly will mark the great day of God's justice and judgment (16:14).

The next statement is directed toward John's audience, the believing community, and presented as the words of Jesus: You will not know when or how I will come, so be alert and ready! (16:15). John's comment about being caught naked (16:15) should not be taken literally, but rather as a metaphor for the believers making themselves vulnerable to shame if they have not properly prepared for Jesus' return. In honor-shame cultures, one's honor is more valuable than any other possession a person might have.

The narrator concludes this vision by saying that the unclean spirits assembled the armies at Armageddon (16:16). In Hebrew, this is *har Megiddo*, which means "mountain of Megiddo." Strategically located between Mount Carmel and the Jordan River in the northern part of Israel, it was the entryway for invading armies from the north and east, and therefore the location of some especially fierce battles in Israel's history. However, for John, Armageddon is not so much a place but a symbol of the battle to end all battles!

Finally the seventh bowl is poured out into the air (16:17). The voice from the temple, the same voice that gave the command for the bowls to be poured out, shouts, "It is done," that is, the full measure of God's wrath is completed (16:17). Again John sees and hears the signs of theophany—thunder, lightning, earthquake, and the sounds that accompany them (16:18). As a result, the great city Babylon (i.e., Rome) was broken into three parts by the earthquake, people were pelted by enormous hailstones weighing a hundred pounds each, and the features of the land were so changed as not to be recognizable anymore (16:19-21). The storm and earthquake were fearful, that is, awesome and of catastrophic proportions! But the

dragon, from the mouth of the beast, and from the mouth of the false prophet. [14]These were demonic spirits who performed signs. They went out to the kings of the whole world to assemble them for the battle on the great day of God the almighty. [15]("Behold, I am coming like a thief." Blessed is the one who watches and keeps his clothes ready, so that he may not go naked and people see him exposed.) [16]They then assembled the kings in the place that is named Armageddon in Hebrew.

[17]The seventh angel poured out his bowl into the air. A loud voice came out of the temple from the throne, saying, "It is done." [18]Then there were lightning flashes, rumblings, and peals of thunder, and a great earthquake. It was such a violent earthquake that there has never been one like it since the human race began on earth. [19]The great city was split into three parts, and the gentile cities fell. But God remembered great Babylon, giving it the cup filled with the wine of his fury and wrath. [20]Every island fled, and mountains disappeared. [21]Large hailstones like huge weights came down from the sky on people, and they blasphemed God for the plague of hail because this plague was so severe.

continue

people did not repent. Rather, their hearts were hardened, so that they cursed God (16:21).

 The plague which envelopes the earth when the fifth bowl is poured out is reminiscent of the ninth plague visited upon the Egyptians in Exodus 10:21-23. The terror which that **plague of unnatural darkness** brought upon the Egyptians is fully explored in Wisdom 17:1–18:4. In prophetic literature, darkness is often associated with the wrath of God and the coming retribution (e.g., Lam 3:1-2; Joel 2:1-2a; Amos 5:18; Ezek 32:7-9; Zeph 1:15).

V: The Punishment of Babylon and the Destruction of Pagan Nations

CHAPTER 17

Babylon the Great

[1]Then one of the seven angels who were holding the seven bowls came and said to me, "Come here. I will show you the judgment on the great harlot who lives near the many waters. [2]The kings of the earth have had intercourse with her, and the inhabitants of the earth became drunk on the wine of her harlotry." [3]Then he carried me away in spirit to a deserted place where I saw a woman seated on a scarlet beast that was covered with blasphemous names, with seven heads and ten horns. [4]The woman was wearing purple and scarlet and adorned with gold, precious stones, and pearls. She held in her hand a gold cup that was filled with the abominable and sordid deeds of her harlotry. [5]On her forehead was written a name, which is a mystery, "Babylon the great, the mother of harlots and of the abominations of the earth." [6]I saw that the woman was drunk on the blood of the holy ones and on the blood of the witnesses to Jesus.

Meaning of the Beast and Harlot

When I saw her I was greatly amazed. [7]The angel said to me, "Why are you amazed? I will explain to you the mystery of the woman and of the beast that carries her, the beast with the seven heads and the ten horns. [8]The beast that you saw existed once but now exists no longer. It will come up from the abyss and is headed for destruction. The inhabitants of the earth whose names have not been written in the book of life from the foundation of the world shall be amazed when they see the beast, because it existed once but exists no longer, and yet it will come again. [9]Here is a clue for one who has wisdom. The seven heads represent seven hills upon which the woman sits. They also represent seven kings: [10]five have already fallen, one still lives, and the last has not yet come, and when he comes he must remain only a short while. [11]The beast that

continue

THE FALL OF BABYLON

Rev 17:1–18:24

Before the book's final series of visions, which describe the judgment of the world and the establishment of God's kingdom, Revelation provides a long interlude in which the judgment against the whore Babylon, that is, Rome, is described in great detail. This topic is not new to the readers of the book of Revelation. The seven bowl visions (16:1-21) that immediately precede this section are a final call to repentance for all who have fallen under the spell of the dragon, that is, Rome, and those who pay allegiance to her. However, Rome's fate was sealed already when the angel-prophet of Revelation 14:8 proclaimed, "Fallen, fallen is Babylon the great." These next two chapters are an elaboration of that prophecy.

17:1-18 Vision of the whore Babylon

The connection with the previous series of bowl visions is established in John's mind by the reappearance of one of the angels who held the seven bowls (17:1). The angel takes John to the wilderness, a place of safety in Revelation 12, but here it is also a vantage point from which he can see everything that is happening on the earth (17:3). From this place the angel invites John to view the verdict issued against the great harlot seated on many waters (17:1).

Although today's reader might be stymied by the metaphor of harlotry, John's readers likely understood that he was referring to the city of Rome. Prostitution and fornication (17:1-2) are metaphoric terms that were regularly used to describe idol worship and the material excesses associated with the Roman Empire (see 2:19-23). Likewise, the phrases "kings of the earth" and "the inhabitants of the earth" (17:2) are symbolic descriptors of those who have pledged allegiance to Rome.

The whore Babylon wears purple, a symbol of royalty, and scarlet, suggesting violence (17:4). The beast on which she rides is the beast of the sea (17:3; see 13:1), previously identified as the Roman Empire. However, now the beast is scarlet, perhaps recalling its connection to the red dragon of Revelation 12. Instead of blasphemous names on its heads (13:1), it now wears *many* blasphemous names *all over its body* (17:3). John continues to describe the harlot, saying that she has a name of mystery on her forehead—Babylon (17:5). The term *mystērion* usually refers to something that is secret or hidden, but in Revelation it also suggests an allegorical interpretation, making Babylon a metaphor for Rome.

 The vision of the **"woman seated on a scarlet beast"** (17:3) recalls to the reader's mind the earlier vision of the "woman clothed with the sun" (12:1). Each figure is the antithesis of the other.

The description of Rome as the one "who lives near the many waters" (17:1), who holds "a gold cup" in her hand (17:4), and whose inhabitants are drunk with the wine of her fornication (Rev 17:2), may be borrowed from Jeremiah's prophecy against Babylon (Jer 51:7, 13). Jeremiah describes Babylon's impending downfall as God's vengeance for the destruction of the temple (Jer 51:11). In the same spirit, the author of the book of Revelation attributes God's vengeance against Rome to its role in the death of the martyrs (17:6).

As John marvels over what he was seeing, one of the angels holding the seven bowls becomes the interpreter of his vision (17:6-7). The angel tells him that the beast is the one "who was and is *not* and is to rise" (17:8; author's translation), an obvious spoof on the name of God in the introduction of the book of Revelation: the one "who is and who was and who is to come" (1:4). If we are correct in assigning Nero's name to the beast in Revelation 13, then the same should apply here. Thus John is saying that Nero was (i.e., he reigned), and is not (i.e., he died), and is to come (i.e., either he or a reign like his will return). See Revelation 13:3 and 13:14. This beast is about to rise from the

"The Lamb will conquer" (Rev 17:14). Mosaic at Church of St. Martin, Brunswick, Germany.

existed once but exists no longer is an eighth king, but really belongs to the seven and is headed for destruction. ¹²The ten horns that you saw represent ten kings who have not yet been crowned; they will receive royal authority along with the beast for one hour. ¹³They are of one mind and will give their power and authority to the beast. ¹⁴They will fight with the Lamb, but the Lamb will conquer them, for he is Lord of lords and king of kings, and those with him are called, chosen, and faithful."

¹⁵Then he said to me, "The waters that you saw where the harlot lives represent large numbers of peoples, nations, and tongues. ¹⁶The ten horns that you saw and the beast will hate the harlot; they will leave her desolate and naked; they will eat her flesh and consume her with fire. ¹⁷For God has put it into their minds to carry out his purpose and to make them come to an agreement to give their kingdom to the beast until the words of God are accomplished. ¹⁸The woman whom you saw represents the great city that has sovereignty over the kings of the earth."

CHAPTER 18

The Fall of Babylon

¹After this I saw another angel coming down from heaven, having great authority, and the earth became illumined by his splendor. ²He cried out in a mighty voice:

"Fallen, fallen is Babylon the great.
   She has become a haunt for demons.

continue

abyss—the place with which it is regularly associated—and is going to perdition—a fate to which it is regularly assigned (17:8; see 11:7). The angel also tells John that the dwellers of the earth who do not have their names in the book of life will marvel over the beast (17:8), presumably because they pay allegiance to the beast and do not associate themselves with the Lamb.

The angel alerts John to pay careful attention to the next part of his interpretation, say-

ing, "Here is a clue for one who has wisdom" (17:9; see 13:8). The "seven hills" are the seven hills on which Rome is seated (17:9). The reader might be tempted to think of the "seven kings" in historical terms, too, but the angel's riddle is vague, and the list of first-century Roman emperors does not correspond to the riddle. At a minimum, we can say that the five fallen kings describe a series of emperors who preceded the currently reigning emperor, the sixth king (17:10). The seventh king will reign for a limited time, and then an eighth will rise to the throne, who is like one of the seven (17:11). Scholars suggest that Nero (the beast personified) is the sixth king and that Domitian (A.D. 81–96) is the eighth king, whom second-century Roman historians described as a tyrant and a megalomaniac. However, little can be said beyond that. It is possible that the seven kings simply signify the full measure of kingship, since seven is the symbol of fullness.

The angel continues his interpretation, explaining that the "ten horns" are the ten kings still to come, who will have authority and be of one mind with the beast (17:12-13). For a short time they will make war on those who are faithful to the Lamb, but in the end the Lamb will be victorious, because he is sovereign over even the most powerful of kings. The ones who are with him need not fear, because they are called and chosen (17:14).

Finally, the angel explains that the "waters" are the peoples of the Roman Empire (17:15). Eventually, the beast and the ten kings who have authority with the beast will turn their hatred on Rome and shame her, devour her, and utterly destroy her (17:16). This is what evil does; it destroys everything, even its own. But as the beast and the kings allied with him rampage, God remains sovereign, because they are actually fulfilling God's purpose and will continue to do so until God's will is accomplished (17:17).

18:1-24 Babylon's fall

John's next vision is of an angel of great authority (18:1-3). The angel apparently originated from beside the heavenly throne, because his reflected glory lights up the earth (18:1). The angel's speech is a prophecy that is delivered in the form of a dirge (i.e., funeral song). The opening statement, "Fallen, fallen is Babylon" (18:2) recalls another angel's prophecy in Revelation 14:8, also against Rome. Rome's fornication involves both idolatry and material excess. The language and imagery of this dirge are similar to that found in Isaiah and Jeremiah (Isa 21:9; Jer 25:15, 27; 50:39).

 The **wanton luxury and wealth** which is a sign of the decadent evil of Babylon/Rome was also denounced by the prophets as a sign of the moral corruption of pre-exilic Israel. The prophet Amos, for example, condemns those "who lie on beds of ivory, / and lounge upon their couches; / Eating lambs taken from the flock, / and calves from the stall; / Who improvise to the music of the harp, / composing on musical instruments like David, / Who drink wine from bowls, / and anoint themselves with the best oils" (6:4-6). The lack of concern displayed by the wealthy is considered to be a clear indicator of the moral decay of the nation.

In addition to the destruction of Rome, the angel prophesies that Rome's vassal kings (18:3) will suffer punishment because they participated in her fornication and will lament her passing (see 18:9-10). Likewise, the merchants of her empire (18:3) will pay a price; they have grown rich on her excess, so they, too, will grieve for her (see 18:11-17). A second voice urges God's people to leave Rome before they are drawn into her sinful ways (18:4; see Isa 48:20; Jer 50:8). Thus John's vision makes clear that sinful activity *will* result in punishment despite appearances to the contrary. Rome revels in her false glory and thinks herself a queen with no reason to mourn, but God remembers her wicked deeds and *in a single day* she will suffer double for her sins (18:5-7). Further, the

She is a cage for every unclean spirit,
  a cage for every unclean bird,
  [a cage for every unclean] and disgusting [beast].
[3]For all the nations have drunk
  the wine of her licentious passion.
The kings of the earth had intercourse with her,
  and the merchants of the earth grew rich
    from her drive for luxury."

[4]Then I heard another voice from heaven say:

"Depart from her, my people,
  so as not to take part in her sins
  and receive a share in her plagues,
[5]for her sins are piled up to the sky,
  and God remembers her crimes.
[6]Pay her back as she has paid others.
  Pay her back double for her deeds.
  Into her cup pour double what she poured.
[7]To the measure of her boasting and
    wantonness
  repay her in torment and grief;
for she said to herself,
  'I sit enthroned as queen;
  I am no widow,
  and I will never know grief.'
[8]Therefore, her plagues will come in one day,
  pestilence, grief, and famine;
  she will be consumed by fire.
For mighty is the Lord God who judges her."

[9]The kings of the earth who had intercourse with her in their wantonness will weep and mourn over her when they see the smoke of her pyre. [10]They will keep their distance for fear of the torment inflicted on her, and they will say:

"Alas, alas, great city,
  Babylon, mighty city.
  In one hour your judgment has come."

[11]The merchants of the earth will weep and mourn for her, because there will be no more markets for their cargo: [12]their cargo of gold, silver, precious stones, and pearls; fine linen, purple silk, and scarlet

continue

cloth; fragrant wood of every kind, all articles of ivory and all articles of the most expensive wood, bronze, iron, and marble; [13]cinnamon, spice, incense, myrrh, and frankincense; wine, olive oil, fine flour, and wheat; cattle and sheep, horses and chariots, and slaves, that is, human beings.

[14]"The fruit you craved
  has left you.
All your luxury and splendor are gone,
  never again will one find them."

[15]The merchants who deal in these goods, who grew rich from her, will keep their distance for fear of the torment inflicted on her. Weeping and mourning, [16]they cry out:

"Alas, alas, great city,
  wearing fine linen, purple and scarlet,
  adorned [in] gold, precious stones, and
    pearls.
[17]In one hour this great wealth has been
    ruined."

Every captain of a ship, every traveler at sea, sailors, and seafaring merchants stood at a distance [18]and cried out when they saw the smoke of her pyre, "What city could compare with the great city?" [19]They threw dust on their heads and cried out, weeping and mourning:

"Alas, alas, great city,
  in which all who had ships at sea
  grew rich from her wealth.
In one hour she has been ruined.
[20]Rejoice over her, heaven,
  you holy ones, apostles, and prophets.
For God has judged your case against her."

[21]A mighty angel picked up a stone like a huge millstone and threw it into the sea and said:

"With such force will Babylon the great city
    be thrown down,
  and will never be found again.

continue

intensity of God's vengeance will demonstrate that the One who judges is sovereign (18:8).

Finally, the angel prophesies that Rome's vassal kings, merchants, and seafarers will mourn over her destruction. Echoing the words of the prophet Ezekiel in his dirge over Tyre, the angel announces that Rome's vassal kings will weep and wail over the once powerful city, their terror rooted in the fact that they deserve the same fate, since they were wanton with her (18:9-10; see Ezek 26:16-17). Likewise, the merchants will mourn because no one buys Rome's riches anymore. All of her luxuries, excesses, and splendid dainties are destroyed, never to be restored (18:12-14; see Ezek 27:12-22). They fear her torment because they became wealthy on account of her (18:15; see Ezek 27:31-36). Finally, the captains of ships, sailors, and sea traders mourn and weep over Rome's burning, because they had grown rich from her wealth (18:17-19; see Ezek 27:30-34).

All three groups express terror over Rome's destruction, not in sympathy with Rome but because of their own self-interest. They understand that they will suffer because Rome suffers. Moreover, all three groups marvel over the swiftness of God's judgment—in a single hour! (18:10, 17, 19). Of course, John's audience would have heard this prophecy of doom as a message of hope, since it asserts unequivocally that God is just, and God's justice, when it comes, will be swift. The message of the prophecy is confirmed, at the conclusion of the lamentations, when John exhorts his hearers—the holy ones, apostles, and prophets—to rejoice because God has given judgment against Rome *on their behalf* (18:20).

Finally, John sees another angel described as "mighty" (18:21). This angel issues a prophecy of doom in both word and action. Taking a stone that resembled a great millstone used for grinding grain into flour, the angel threw it into the sea, where it quickly sank to the bottom. "With such force shall Babylon the great city be thrown down," the angel says, "and will never be found again" (18:21). Thus begins a litany whose antiphon is "No . . . will ever be heard in you again" (18:22-23).

What are these things that will no longer be seen or heard in Rome? They are the instruments of joy and merriment, the craftspeople that sustain the quality of life of the society (18:22), the grinding stones that help put bread on the table (18:22), the lights that brighten people's homes (18:23), and the bride and bridegroom whose marriage provides offspring for the future (18:23). As a literary technique, the litany booms like a solemn drumbeat or death knell: Rome will be no more! Finally, the mighty angel reveals the reason for this massive and pervasive destruction: the merchants deceived people with their sorcery and, more importantly, the blood of the martyrs was found in the great city that was Rome (18:24). In other words, God is about to avenge the death of his holy ones!

> ²²No melodies of harpists and musicians,
>   flutists and trumpeters,
>   will ever be heard in you again.
> No craftsmen in any trade
>   will ever be found in you again.
> No sound of the millstone
>   will ever be heard in you again.
> ²³No light from a lamp
>   will ever be seen in you again.
> No voices of bride and groom
>   will ever be heard in you again.
> Because your merchants were the great ones
>   of the world,
>   all nations were led astray by your magic
>   potion.
> ²⁴In her was found the blood of prophets and
>   holy ones
>   and all who have been slain on the earth."

 Numbers are used liberally throughout the book of Revelation, and readers sometimes mistakenly take them literally rather than symbolically, as they are intended by the author. Here are the most commonly cited numbers and their symbolic meanings.

Number	Symbolic Meaning
Three	A number suggesting a few, a limited number, or a limited time.
Four	Fullness, especially as it relates to the breadth of the universe (e.g., four corners of the world); universality.
Seven	Perfection, fullness, perfect orderedness. In the book of Genesis, it is the number of the completeness of creation.
Ten	Sometimes denoting a limited number, other times recalling the ten kings of Daniel 7:24, who oppress the holy ones of God in the period before God's reign is finally established. Can also symbolize fullness or completeness.
Twelve	Fullness or completeness, especially bringing diversity into unity. Israel was made up of twelve tribes. The calendar year consists of twelve months, and the day has two sets of twelve hours.
Thousand	A number signifying myriads, a number too large to count.

EXPLORING LESSON SIX

1. Reflect for a few minutes on your study of Revelation thus far. What are you enjoying about Revelation? What are you finding especially meaningful? What is most challenging for you about this book?

_____

_____

_____

_____

_____

_____

2. Read the songs of Moses in Exodus 15:1-18 and Deuteronomy 32:3-4. How is the martyrs' song in Revelation 15:2-4 similar?

_____

_____

_____

_____

_____

_____

3. a) What is the goal of God's fury (16:1-9)?

_____

_____

_____

_____

_____

b) What Exodus event is John recalling with the seven bowls image? (See Exod 7–11.)

_____

_____

_____

_____

_____

4. How does the image of the thief and the blessing that follows help shape your understanding of God's final judgment (16:15)? (See Matt 24:42-44; 1 Thess 5:1-6.)

_____

_____

_____

_____

_____

5. a) What is the meaning of the word "Armageddon," and what is its historical significance?

_____

_____

_____

_____

   b) What is the symbolic meaning of Armageddon for John (16:16)? (See Judg 5:19-20; 2 Kgs 23:29-30.)

_____

_____

_____

_____

6. John alerts readers to pay special attention to the angel's interpretation of the beast (17:9). How and in what circumstances does God get your attention?

_____

_____

_____

_____

_____

7. What do we learn about God's sovereignty in 17:9-14? (See 1 Tim 6:13-16.)

_____

_____

_____

_____

_____

8. As a whole, chapters 17 and 18 highlight Rome's evil ways. In what ways, if any, can the label "Babylon" can be applied to our civilization today?

_____

_____

_____

_____

_____

_____

9. How do you feel about the sense of vengeance that appears in 18:6-8 and other biblical passages (e.g., Isa 34:8; Jer 50:15; Nah 1:2)? Why do you think the Bible includes such passages?

_____

_____

_____

_____

_____

_____

10. Why are the merchants of earth mourning (18:11-17)? (See Ezek 26:16-17; 27:12-22, 31-36.)

_____

_____

_____

_____

_____

CLOSING PRAYER

Prayer

"Great and wonderful are your works,
Lord God almighty.
Just and true are your ways,
O king of the nations."   (Rev 15:3)

Lord God, you are the Almighty, the just and the true. I am quick to turn to you with my needs, but less likely to raise my voice in praise. Give me the wisdom to recognize your glory. Inspire me to give thanks for your blessings and presence. May I glorify you today by my words and actions, praising you especially for . . .

LESSON SEVEN

Revelation 19–22

Begin your personal study and group discussion with a simple and sincere prayer such as:

Prayer

Heavenly Father, you are the Alpha and the Omega, our beginning and end. As we study the revelation given to your servant John, inspire us with hope in your promises and the strength to stay faithful to you always.

Read the Bible text of Revelation 19–22 found in the outside columns of pages 100–109, highlighting what stands out to you.

Read the accompanying commentary to add to your understanding.

Respond to the questions on pages 111–113, Exploring Lesson Seven.

The Closing Prayer on page 114 is for your personal use and may be used at the end of group discussion.

CHAPTER 19

¹After this I heard what sounded like the loud voice of a great multitude in heaven, saying:

"Alleluia!
Salvation, glory, and might belong to our God,
²for true and just are his judgments.
He has condemned the great harlot
who corrupted the earth with her harlotry.
He has avenged on her the blood of his
servants."

³They said a second time:

"Alleluia! Smoke will rise from her forever
and ever."

⁴The twenty-four elders and the four living creatures fell down and worshiped God who sat on the throne, saying, "Amen. Alleluia."

The Victory Song

⁵A voice coming from the throne said:

"Praise our God, all you his servants,
[and] you who revere him, small and great."

⁶Then I heard something like the sound of a great multitude or the sound of rushing water or mighty peals of thunder, as they said:

"Alleluia!
The Lord has established his reign,
[our] God, the almighty.
⁷Let us rejoice and be glad
and give him glory.
For the wedding day of the Lamb has come,
his bride has made herself ready.
⁸She was allowed to wear
a bright, clean linen garment."

(The linen represents the righteous deeds of the holy ones.)

⁹Then the angel said to me, "Write this: Blessed are those who have been called to the wedding feast of the Lamb." And he said to me, "These words are true; they come from God." ¹⁰I fell at

continue

SEVEN VISIONS OF THE LAST THINGS

Rev 19:1–20:15

The book of Revelation concludes with a final series of visions that describe the judgment that is about to come upon the wicked and the reward that is promised to the righteous. All of these visions are presented in highly mythical language. Therefore, they should be interpreted as symbolic and not historical descriptions. However, the message is clear: God is just and God is sovereign. God will *indeed* vindicate the righteous and punish the wicked.

19:1-10 The heavenly liturgy

As a prelude to the visions of the last things, once again John is allowed to witness the heavenly liturgy (cf. 7:9-12; 14:1-5). The great multitude (19:1) described here is apparently the same as the great multitude who earlier stood before God's throne, dressed in white robes and with palm branches in their hands (cf. 7:9). They shout, "Alleluia," which translates "Praise Yʜᴡʜ," and they sing a song of victory on account of God's true and just condemnation of the whore Babylon, i.e., Rome, and God's avenging of the death of the martyrs (19:2-3; cf. 6:10). Again, they shout "Alleluia" and affirm the final end of Rome by saying that the smoke from the city goes up forever and ever (19:3). John's mention of the twenty-four elders and the four living creatures who joined in worship of God, who is seated on the throne, again recalls the throne vision of Revelation 4.

Suddenly a voice from the throne calls everyone in heaven to offer praise to God (19:5), and the multitude responds with a sound so deafening that it resembles rushing water and thunder crashing (19:6). Again, they shout "Alleluia" and assert that God, the Almighty One, reigns as king (19:6), and they announce with great joy that it is time for the marriage of the Lamb. The bride, whose identity has not yet been revealed, has completed her wedding preparations (19:7). Her bridal gown, which is made of fine, costly, bright white linen (a type found only in Egypt), symbolizes her holiness (19:8). The gown *is given* (passive verb form) to her, meaning that it is a gift *from God* and God is the source or cause of her holiness. John adds that the bridal gown is the righteous deeds of the holy ones (19:8; cf. 15:6). Therefore, we can conclude that the bride is a metaphor for the church, and the holy ones are the members of the church. For a long time they waited under God's altar, demanding God's vengeance on those who killed them (6:9-11). Now they rejoice because the time of God's vindication has finally come (19:6-7).

John goes on to say that he heard the voice from the throne tell him to write the very words of God, "Blessed are those who have been called to the wedding feast of the Lamb" (19:9). This beatitude is about the establishment of God's kingdom, and being *the very words of God*, it carries divine authority. Elsewhere in the New Testament, imagery of a marriage feast is likewise associated with the coming of God's kingdom (Matt 22:1-14; 25:1-13).

John falls down to worship the angel, but the angel stops him, telling him that he is not a deity. Rather, he is a fellow servant who holds the testimony of (i.e., concerning) Jesus (19:10). The Greek is difficult to translate into English here, but basically the angel is saying that he, like John himself and others like him, is a prophet who witnesses to Jesus by speaking

his feet to worship him. But he said to me, "Don't! I am a fellow servant of yours and of your brothers who bear witness to Jesus. Worship God. Witness to Jesus is the spirit of prophecy."

The King of Kings

[11]Then I saw the heavens opened, and there was a white horse; its rider was [called] "Faithful and True." He judges and wages war in righteousness. [12]His eyes were [like] a fiery flame, and on his head were many diadems. He had a name inscribed that no one knows except himself. [13]He wore a cloak that had been dipped in blood, and his name was called the Word of God. [14]The armies of heaven followed him, mounted on white horses and wearing clean white linen. [15]Out

continue

his word (19:10; cf. 1:1-3). But they must worship only God! (19:10).

After this glorious vision of heavenly worship, John witnesses in rapid succession seven visions of vindication and final judgment. These are all cosmic in scope, embracing heaven and earth and even the space under the earth. The imagery is extremely graphic, but it should not be taken literally. Rather, using metaphorical language, John is asserting that God is sovereign and just and that God rewards the righteous and punishes the wicked.

19:11-16 Vision of the white horse and rider

In the first of seven concluding visions, John sees heaven opened, and again a white horse and rider appear. However, this time the rider is not the Parthian army that made war on Rome (6:2); this one is "Faithful and True" (19:11; cf. 3:14). Because he is described as having eyes of fire with a sword coming from his mouth (19:12, 15), the reader should conclude that the rider is the risen Jesus of the initial vision of this book (see 1:14, 16). He rides a beast of war, the horse, but his is a war of righteousness (19:11). The "many of his mouth came a sharp sword to strike the nations. He will rule them with an iron rod, and he himself will tread out in the wine press the wine of the fury and wrath of God the almighty. ¹⁶He has a name written on his cloak and on his thigh, "King of kings and Lord of lords."

¹⁷Then I saw an angel standing on the sun. He cried out [in] a loud voice to all the birds flying high overhead, "Come here. Gather for God's great feast, ¹⁸to eat the flesh of kings, the flesh of military officers, and the flesh of warriors, the flesh of horses and of their riders, and the flesh of all, free and slave, small and great." ¹⁹Then I saw the beast and the kings of the earth and their armies gathered to fight against the one riding the horse and against his army. ²⁰The beast was caught and with it the false prophet who had performed in its sight the signs by which he led astray those who had accepted the mark of the beast and those who had worshiped its image. The two were thrown alive into the fiery pool burning with sulfur. ²¹The rest were killed by the sword that came out of the mouth of the one riding the horse, and all the birds gorged themselves on their flesh.

continue

diadems" on his head (19:12) signify supreme kingship. Recall that the dragon wore seven diadems (12:3), and the beast wore ten (13:1). The "name . . . that no one knows" (19:12) means that he has absolute authority, and no one has ownership over him (19:12; cf. 14:1; 17:5), though later he is identified as "Word of God" (19:13), which symbolizes divine authority. The blood-washed robe (19:13) is a symbol of victory in battle (Isa 63:1-3; Wis 18:14-16), and "tread[ing] the wine press" (19:15) describes the wrath of God on judgment day—God will crush the wicked so hard that their lifeblood will spurt out and run like a river! (see Isa 63:1-3). The heavenly army of the risen Jesus is also victorious, dressed in white linen robes (19:14), much like those of the bride in the preceding vision (cf. 7:9). These are the martyrs who had washed their robes in the blood of the Lamb and now no longer hunger or thirst or suffer grief (cf. 7:9-17).

19:17-18 Vision of the great supper of God

The second vision takes place in the mid-heaven (i.e., the sky). An angel standing in the sun invites all the birds of the sky to enjoy God's banquet (19:17). The banquet imagery is borrowed from Ezekiel's prophecy against Gog of the land of Magog (Ezek 39:17-20) and is typical of apocalyptic literature. However, for the novice reader, the imagery can be appalling! The birds are invited to dine on the flesh of kings, captains, soldiers, horses, and riders (19:18). Imagine the perverse delight of John's audience, thinking about how their persecutors would be eaten alive—banquet food for birds of prey! Thus God punishes the wicked.

19:19-21 Vision of the destruction of the beast and the false prophet

Without transition, suddenly John observes the beast and the kings of the earth gathering for battle against the Word of God and his army (19:19). This is the preparation for Armageddon (see 16:16). But the war is swift. The beast and the false prophet—the beasts of Revelation 13—are captured without incident, suggesting that they have little power when confronted by the risen Christ and the army of God (19:20). The lake of fire into which they are thrown symbolizes their final destruction (19:20). The slaying of the "rest" (19:21) explains how the kings, military officers, warriors, horses, and riders came to be table fare for God's banquet. Later they, too, will be thrown into the lake of fire (see 20:15).

20:1-10 The "thousand-year" visions

The fourth and fifth visions in this series are sandwiched together into an intercalation. The seer John begins by narrating the first part of the outer vision, then breaks away to describe the inner vision, and finally returns to complete the narration of the outer vision. The reader should think of the two visions as taking place at the same time. While the inner vision takes place in heaven, the outer vision spans all three realms of the created world.

In the outer vision (20:1-3, 7-10), the dragon (see Rev 12) is taken captive by the angel who descends from heaven with the key to the bottomless pit (see Rev 9). The angel hurls the dragon into the pit and seals it for a thousand years (20:2-3). Note the three other names by which the dragon is known: the ancient serpent, the Devil, and Satan (20:2; cf. 12:9). The dragon's capture marks the end of his "short while" on earth (cf. 12:12). But this is not *the* end, for John is told that the dragon must be released for a little while after the thousand years are finished (20:3). The verb of necessity, *dei* in Greek, suggests that this is part of God's plan. Therefore God's holy ones should not be fearful.

Leaving the reader in suspense about the dragon, John abruptly shifts to the fifth vision (20:4-6), the thousand-year reign of Christ and those who had been martyred in his name. John sees thrones and, seated upon them, the ones who were given authority to judge (20:4). These are the souls of those who were martyred for their testimony to Jesus. God rewards them with resurrection so that they can share in Christ's reign (20:4). This, the reader learns, is the first resurrection (20:5). Those who enjoy the first resurrection are blessed because the second death (i.e., the general judgment, here associated with the lake of fire) will bring them no harm (20:6). Thus John asserts that God is just and God will reward the righteous.

Finally, John returns to the second half of the fourth vision (20:7-10). Satan is now released from his thousand-year bondage to gather his armies from the four corners of the earth (20:7). John's reference to Gog and Magog (20:8) comes from Ezekiel 38, in which the prophet rails against Gog, the king of Magog, who came from the far northern regions to wage war against Israel. The prophet promises that God's wrath will fall on Gog, and he and his armies will be utterly destroyed. Why? It is to show that God is great and holy and to make God known to the whole world! (Ezek 38:23). Here John describes Magog not as Gog's kingdom but as a person who is in alliance with Gog. However,

CHAPTER 20

The Thousand-year Reign

¹Then I saw an angel come down from heaven, holding in his hand the key to the abyss and a heavy chain. ²He seized the dragon, the ancient serpent, which is the Devil or Satan, and tied it up for a thousand years ³and threw it into the abyss, which he locked over it and sealed, so that it could no longer lead the nations astray until the thousand years are completed. After this, it is to be released for a short time.

⁴Then I saw thrones; those who sat on them were entrusted with judgment. I also saw the souls of those who had been beheaded for their witness to Jesus and for the word of God, and who had not worshiped the beast or its image nor had accepted its mark on their foreheads or hands. They came to life and they reigned with Christ for a thousand years. ⁵The rest of the dead did not come to life until the thousand years were over.

continue

the message is the same as Ezekiel's: God is sovereign, and God will destroy the wicked.

 The **thousand-year reign** (Rev 20) has fascinated interpreters for generations and has fueled a movement known as millenarianism (or millennialism). Although its roots go back to the early church, modern versions of it exist among some fundamentalist Christians who envision the thousand-year reign as lasting literally one thousand years, either before or after the second coming of Christ. Most interpreters, however, understand the "thousand years" as representative of a suitably long period of time—a time when victory has been declared (by the death and resurrection of Christ) but is not yet final. In the end, God's victory will be definitive, establishing a lasting kingdom of justice and peace.

This is the first resurrection. ⁶Blessed and holy is the one who shares in the first resurrection. The second death has no power over these; they will be priests of God and of Christ, and they will reign with him for [the] thousand years.

⁷When the thousand years are completed, Satan will be released from his prison. ⁸He will go out to deceive the nations at the four corners of the earth, Gog and Magog, to gather them for battle; their number is like the sand of the sea. ⁹They invaded the breadth of the earth and surrounded the camp of the holy ones and the beloved city. But fire came down from heaven and consumed them. ¹⁰The Devil who had led them astray was thrown into the pool of fire and sulfur, where the beast and the false prophet were. There they will be tormented day and night forever and ever.

The Large White Throne

¹¹Next I saw a large white throne and the one who was sitting on it. The earth and the sky fled from his presence and there was no place for them. ¹²I saw the dead, the great and the lowly, standing before the throne, and scrolls were opened. Then another scroll was opened, the book of life. The dead were judged according to their deeds, by what was written in the scrolls. ¹³The sea gave up its

continue

With his vast armies coming from all over the world, Satan is ready to make war against God's people (20:8). John's use of the phrase "camp of the holy ones" (20:9) may be intended to recall the wilderness camp of the Israelites during the Exodus (e.g., Exod 19:16-17). The "beloved city" is Jerusalem (20:9). The holy ones are the members of the church (20:9). This is the battle of Armageddon, which John first mentioned in 16:14-16 and again in 17:14 and 19:11-21. The name is derived from the Hebrew *har Megiddo*, which means "mountain of Megiddo." Historically, it was the location of some of Israel's fiercest battles. Here it takes on cosmic and mythical proportions. The battle is swift and decisive! God intervenes on behalf of the holy ones, sending fire on the earth (20:9; cf. Ezek 38:22). Satan is thrown into the lake of fire, where the beast and the false prophet have already met their end (20:10).

20:11-15 Vision of judgment before God's throne

This throne vision has a link back to the fifth vision of the last things, in which the martyrs are described as seated on thrones in order to share judgment with the risen Christ (20:4), but it also recalls the throne vision of Revelation 4. Thus, as we arrive at the end of the book of Revelation, we have come full circle to a vision of the sovereign God seated on the throne

 Revelation and the Afterlife

Revelation is a book about God's ultimate victory over evil. Christ, the victorious Lamb, will conquer all evil and establish an endless reign of justice and peace. But the message of victory is accompanied by a warning: those who do not repent of their sinfulness here and now may face eternal condemnation, "the second death" (20:6, 14; see also 2:11; 21:8). This warning is not unique to Revelation. Jesus' preaching in the Gospels also calls for repentance and conversion so as to avoid eternal damnation (e.g., Matt 13:40-43; Mark 9:43-48).

The image of fiery condemnation most likely originates in the stark reality of the garbage dump outside the city walls of Jerusalem known as "Gehenna" (see Matt 10:28; 23:33; Luke 12:5; Jas 3:6). By New Testament times, the smelly, fiery, smoldering reality had become the primary symbol for a place of punishment and life without God's presence, that is, hell.

Like many difficult topics and ideas in the book of Revelation, we are left to grapple with its dire warnings about the afterlife. One thing is clear: what we do with our lives here and now makes a difference in the life to come (Rev 20:12-13; 22:12; see also Matt 25:31-46; 1 Thess 1:7-10).

of glory. Given the pervasiveness of the parallel theme of God's justice, the reader should not be surprised that this sixth (and second to the last) vision is one of judgment.

God's throne is white (20:11), signifying victory over the forces of evil. The earth and sky have fled (20:11), presumably because nothing tainted by evil can exist in this holy place, but also in anticipation of the final vision of this book, the New Jerusalem (see 21:1–22:5). Then John sees the dead as they emerge from the sea and the underworld (Hades) to stand before God, who will judge them based upon what is contained in the book of deeds and the book of life (20:12-13). Some, though not all, first-century Jews believed in a general resurrection of the dead at the end time, in which people would be judged on the basis of their deeds (see, for example, Dan 7:10). In this vision those whose names are not in the book of life are sentenced to the second death, the lake of fire (20:15). When the general judgment of human beings is complete, Death (personified; the consequence of evil) and Hades (the place of the dead) are also thrown into the lake of fire (20:14). John does not mention the fate of the holy ones, because they already enjoy resurrection with Christ (see 20:6). Thus John asserts God's power over the forces of evil and his justice in punishing the wicked. In sum, the slate has been wiped clean for the transformed *cosmos* (universe), which is about to appear.

VISION OF THE NEW JERUSALEM

Rev 21:1–22:5

The vision of the New Jerusalem is the seventh in this sequence of visions of the last things and the final vision of the book of Revelation. It can be divided into three parts based upon the three images used to describe this transformed universe: the bride and wife of the Lamb (21:1-8), the new temple (21:9-27), and the new creation (22:1-5).

21:1-8 The bride and wife of the Lamb

In the preceding vision (20:11-15), John narrated a scene in which the palette of God's crea-

dead; then Death and Hades gave up their dead. All the dead were judged according to their deeds. ¹⁴Then Death and Hades were thrown into the pool of fire. (This pool of fire is the second death.) ¹⁵Anyone whose name was not found written in the book of life was thrown into the pool of fire.

VI: The New Creation

CHAPTER 21

The New Heaven and the New Earth

¹Then I saw a new heaven and a new earth. The former heaven and the former earth had passed away, and the sea was no more. ²I also saw the holy city, a new Jerusalem, coming down out of heaven from God, prepared as a bride adorned for her husband. ³I heard a loud voice from the throne saying, "Behold, God's dwelling is with the human race. He will dwell with them and they will be his people and God himself will always be with them [as their God]. ⁴He will wipe every tear from their eyes, and there shall be no more death or mourning, wailing or pain, [for] the old order has passed away."

⁵The one who sat on the throne said, "Behold, I make all things new." Then he said, "Write these words down, for they are trustworthy and true." ⁶He said to me, "They are accomplished. I [am] the Alpha and the Omega, the beginning and the end. To the thirsty I will give a gift from the spring of life-giving water. ⁷The victor will inherit these gifts, and I shall be his God, and he will be my son. ⁸But

continue

tion has been wiped clean. Now he sees a *new* heaven and a *new* earth and the holy city, a *new* Jerusalem, coming out of heaven from God (21:1-2). The reader should notice that this vision is not about the coming of an otherworldly reality, but the restoration of a transformed *this*-worldly reality. John compares it to a bride who has prepared herself for her husband (21:2). The imagery is traditional. The prophets of the Old Testament used the bridal image to describe the restoration of the historical Jerusalem, when as for cowards, the unfaithful, the depraved, murderers, the unchaste, sorcerers, idol-worshipers, and deceivers of every sort, their lot is in the burning pool of fire and sulfur, which is the second death."

The New Jerusalem

⁹One of the seven angels who held the seven bowls filled with the seven last plagues came and said to me, "Come here. I will show you the bride, the wife of the Lamb." ¹⁰He took me in spirit to a great, high mountain and showed me the holy city Jerusalem coming down out of heaven from God. ¹¹It gleamed with the splendor of God. Its radiance was like that of a precious stone, like jasper, clear as crystal. ¹²It had a massive, high wall, with twelve gates where twelve angels were stationed and on which names were inscribed, [the names] of the twelve tribes of the Israelites. ¹³There were three gates facing east, three north, three south, and three west. ¹⁴The wall of the city had twelve courses of stones as its foundation, on which were inscribed the twelve names of the twelve apostles of the Lamb.

continue

God's people would return from the Babylonian exile. See, for example, Isaiah 49:18: "Look about and see, / they are all gathering and coming to you. / As I live—oracle of the Lord— / you shall don them as jewels, / bedeck yourself like a bride." See also Isaiah 52:1 and Isaiah 61:10.

The voice that John hears explains the significance of the vision: this is God's dwelling, and the people who reside in this city are God's people (21:3). The relationship, which the voice describes, is *covenant*. The language is almost identical to that of Ezekiel: "I will make a covenant of peace with them . . . . My dwelling shall be with them; I will be their God, and they will be my people" (Ezek 37:26-27). As narrated in the previous vision (20:11-15), the old order, dominated by the dragon, the beasts of the land and sea, Death and Hades, has passed away. Therefore there is no suffering or death

in this new order (21:4). This, too, is traditional imagery for the restoration of Jerusalem. See, for example, Isaiah 25:7-8: "On this mountain . . . the Lord God will wipe away the tears from all faces."

Now God speaks: "They are accomplished," that is, "the transformation is complete" (21:6; see 21:5). God's declaration, "I [am] the Alpha and the Omega" (the first and last letters of the Greek alphabet; 21:6), is an assertion of sovereignty over all things. Thus God promises to the thirsty (i.e., those who have committed themselves in covenant with God) the water of life *as a gift* and reaffirms his covenant with the holy ones (21:6-7). Again, the imagery is traditional. See, for example, Isaiah 55:1, 3: "All you who are thirsty, / come to the water! / You who have no money, / Come, buy grain without money, / . . . / I will make with you an everlasting covenant, / the steadfast loyalty promised to David." Other examples of water associated with life in the messianic age include Isaiah 41:17-18; Isaiah 44:3-4; Ezekiel 47:1-12; Zechariah 13:1; and Zechariah 14:8. The phrase to "the victor" (21:7) recalls the promises at the conclusion of the letters to the seven churches in Revelation 2–3. The reference to those who are doomed for the lake of fire (21:8) is a reminder that nothing evil can reside in this transformed city, the bride of the Lamb.

21:9-27 The new temple

When one of the angels of the seven plagues approaches John and invites him to see the bride of the Lamb (21:9), John is transported to a high mountain—most likely the location of the historical Jerusalem—where he can see the New Jerusalem coming out of heaven from God (21:10). In ancient Judaism the Jerusalem temple was the symbol of God's covenant, its worship center, and the place where God's glory resides on earth. Here John will use the temple as a metaphor for the New Jerusalem.

Again, the imagery is traditional. The new city is radiant with God's glory (21:11; cf. Isa 60:1-2; Ezek 43:2-5; Zech 2:9). Its cubic shape mirrors the holy of holies in Solomon's temple (21:16; cf. 1 Kgs 6:20; 2 Chr 3:8f.), and the plan of the temple, including its three gates on each of four walls, recalls Ezekiel's plan of the temple (21:12-13; cf. Ezek 41:21-22; 43:16; 45:1; 48:20). The twelve precious stones of the foundation of the walls (21:19) recall the high priest's breastplate, which was to have twelve stones representing the twelve tribes (cf. Exod 28:17-21). They also recall the promise of Jerusalem's restoration contained in both Tobit and Isaiah (Tob 13:15-17; Isa 54:11-12).

Some of the details of John's vision remind the reader that although the New Jerusalem is this-worldly, it also has a cosmic and mythical dimension. Its walls, for example, measure 144 cubits in height and thickness (21:17). A cubit was measured from the elbow to the tip of one's finger, approximately 18 inches, so 144 cubits is approximately 72 yards. More importantly, 144 is the total of 12 multiplied by 12, or perfection squared. Since the city walls were its first line of protection against attackers, this one is perfectly protected! The city itself measures four-square, 12,000 *stadia* on a side and 12,000 *stadia* high (21:16). A *stadion* measured approximately 606 feet, so 12,000 *stadia* is approximately 1,377 miles. A city this size is not feasible, but the symbolism is important. A four-square city, characterized by perfection (12) multiplied by a number too great to count (1,000), suggests one that is perfect in its dimensions, comprehensive, and all-inclusive. Consistent with this view of the city is the description of its walls being made of jasper, its streets paved in gold, and each of its gates crafted of a single pearl! (21:18, 21).

Other details in John's vision of the New Jerusalem are reminiscent of the throne vision of Revelation 4. For example, the city having the radiance of jasper (21:11) recalls the description of the One seated on the throne, who appeared "like jasper and carnelian" (4:3). Likewise, the names of the twelve tribes of Israel inscribed on the gates of the city (21:12) and the names of the twelve apostles inscribed on the foundation stones (21:14) recall the twenty-four elders who were situated on thrones surrounding the throne of God (4:4). Thus the reader should not be surprised when John announces that he saw

[15]The one who spoke to me held a gold measuring rod to measure the city, its gates, and its wall. [16]The city was square, its length the same as [also] its width. He measured the city with the rod and found it fifteen hundred miles in length and width and height. [17]He also measured its wall: one hundred and forty-four cubits according to the standard unit of measurement the angel used. [18]The wall was constructed of jasper, while the city was pure gold, clear as glass. [19]The foundations of the city wall were decorated with every precious stone; the first course of stones was jasper, the second sapphire, the third chalcedony, the fourth emerald, [20]the fifth sardonyx, the sixth carnelian, the seventh chrysolite, the eighth beryl, the ninth topaz, the tenth chrysoprase, the eleventh hyacinth, and the twelfth amethyst. [21]The twelve gates were twelve pearls, each of the gates made from a single pearl; and the street of the city was of pure gold, transparent as glass.

[22]I saw no temple in the city, for its temple is the Lord God almighty and the Lamb. [23]The city had no need of sun or moon to shine on it, for the glory of God gave it light, and its lamp was the Lamb. [24]The nations will walk by its light, and to it the kings of the earth will bring their treasure. [25]During the day its gates will never be shut, and there will be no night there. [26]The treasure and wealth of the nations will be brought there, [27]but nothing unclean will enter it, nor any[one] who does abominable things or tells lies. Only those will enter whose names are written in the Lamb's book of life.

continue

no temple in the new city. God and the Lamb reside directly—that is, without the mediation of a temple—in the city (21:22). God's glory and the radiance of the Lamb provide the city's light, and because God is forever faithful, there is no need to fear danger because the city will never have darkness in it (21:23, 25). Moreover, God's radiance will attract all nations into the city, and nothing unclean will enter it (21:24, 26-27). In sum, the New Jerusalem is God's dwelling place on earth.

CHAPTER 22

[1]Then the angel showed me the river of life-giving water, sparkling like crystal, flowing from the throne of God and of the Lamb [2]down the middle of its street. On either side of the river grew the tree of life that produces fruit twelve times a year, once each month; the leaves of the trees serve as medicine for the nations. [3]Nothing accursed will be found there anymore. The throne of God and of the Lamb will be in it, and his servants will worship him. [4]They will look upon his face, and his name will be on their foreheads. [5]Night will be no more, nor will they need light from lamp or sun, for the Lord God shall give them light, and they shall reign forever and ever.

VII: Epilogue

[6]And he said to me, "These words are trustworthy and true, and the Lord, the God of prophetic spirits, sent his angel to show his servants what must happen soon." [7]"Behold, I am coming soon." Blessed is the one who keeps the prophetic message of this book.

[8]It is I, John, who heard and saw these things, and when I heard and saw them I fell down to worship at the feet of the angel who showed them to me. [9]But he said to me, "Don't! I am a fellow servant of yours and of your brothers the prophets and of those who keep the message of this book. Worship God."

[10]Then he said to me, "Do not seal up the prophetic words of this book, for the appointed time is near. [11]Let the wicked still act wickedly, and the filthy still be filthy. The righteous must still do right, and the holy still be holy."

continue

22:1-5 The new creation

In the third segment of this vision, the angel of the seven plagues takes John to see the river of the water of life coming out of the throne of God and the Lamb, which is now inside of the city (22:1). Again, the imagery is traditional. The river recalls the second creation story in Genesis, which provided the setting for God's creation of a human from the dust of the earth (cf. Gen 2:9-10), as well as Ezekiel's vision of a river of water flowing from the temple (Ezek 47:1-12) and Zechariah's vision of water coming from Jerusalem when God's day of judgment comes (Zech 14:8). John's observation that there is a tree of life on each side of the river (22:2) recalls the tree of life that God placed in the garden, also from the second creation story (cf. Gen 2:9). It is the same tree from which Adam and Eve were banished after their sin (Gen 3:22). In other words, John's vision of the New Jerusalem is paradise restored!

John further observes that these trees produce fruit twelve months of the year, and they have leaves that are good for healing of the nations (22:2). The language is closely related to that of the prophet Ezekiel: "[T]heir leaves will not wither, nor will their fruit fail. Every month they will bear fresh fruit because the waters of the river flow out from the sanctuary. Their fruit is used for food, and their leaves for healing" (Ezek 47:12). The point of this part of the vision: God will provide all they need for nourishment and for well-being. John adds "for *the nations*," making the vision all-inclusive (emphasis added). John's observation that there is nothing accursed in the city (22:3) and no darkness (22:5) recalls an end-time prophecy about the lifting of the curse on Jerusalem, so that it can finally live in safety (cf. Zech 14:7-11). In sum, John's vision of the New Jerusalem is the establishment of a new creation, or better, a return to the first creation, before there was sin and evil in the world. It is a return to the Garden of Eden.

CONCLUDING MATERIALS

Rev 22:6-21

Revelation ends with a collection of warnings, beatitudes, and exhortations, some of which recall earlier sections of the book. Several refer to the prophetic character of the book.

The heavenly being who is speaking to John (22:6) appears at first to be one of the seven angels who hold the seven bowls (21:9). However, some of the later sayings in this section

Christ Pantokrator ("Almighty"), Deësis Mosaic, Hagia Sophia, Istanbul

[12]"Behold, I am coming soon. I bring with me the recompense I will give to each according to his deeds. [13]I am the Alpha and the Omega, the first and the last, the beginning and the end."

[14]Blessed are they who wash their robes so as to have the right to the tree of life and enter the city through its gates. [15]Outside are the dogs, the sorcerers, the unchaste, the murderers, the idol-worshipers, and all who love and practice deceit.

[16]"I, Jesus, sent my angel to give you this testimony for the churches. I am the root and offspring of David, the bright morning star."

[17]The Spirit and the bride say, "Come." Let the hearer say, "Come." Let the one who thirsts come forward, and the one who wants it receive the gift of life-giving water.

[18]I warn everyone who hears the prophetic words in this book: if anyone adds to them, God will add to him the plagues described in this book, [19]and if anyone takes away from the words in this prophetic book, God will take away his share in the tree of life and in the holy city described in this book.

[20]The one who gives this testimony says, "Yes, I am coming soon." Amen! Come, Lord Jesus!

[21]The grace of the Lord Jesus be with all.

are clearly those of the risen Christ (e.g., 22:12-13). Perhaps we have sayings from a variety of sources, without regard to the identity of the speaker, collected together at the end of this document. The description of these words as "trustworthy and true" (22:6) is an assertion of their authenticity, as is the statement that God sent his angel to tell his prophets what must take place soon (22:6). John made a similar statement in the opening of the book (see 1:1).

The declaration "I am coming soon" (22:7) most likely comes from the risen Christ (cf. 3:11). It will appear two more times in this section, in 22:12 and 22:20. The beatitude about keeping the message of this book is a short form of the first beatitude of the book of Revelation (1:3).

Now John speaks, identifying himself again as the recipient of the revelation (22:8; cf. 1:1, 9). He also recalls his encounter with the angel messenger in 19:10, with a few variations: the "brothers" of the earlier recollection are now "the prophets," and "the witness to Jesus" is now "the message of this book."

This next saying is directed to John and most likely comes from the angel of verse 6. The command *not* to seal the words of the book

(22:10) signals the immediacy of the end (cf. Dan 8:26). The saying about letting the wicked still act wickedly may sound like determinism, but since the book of Revelation allows for the possibility of repentance (see, for example, 14:6), that interpretation is unlikely. Instead, we should understand it as a warning not to be complacent but always to be ready, for the end is near.

The saying that begins "I am coming soon" (22:12) signals that the risen Christ is now speaking and that he brings rewards for believers according to their works. The attribution "Alpha and Omega" (22:13) is used elsewhere in the book of Revelation only for God (1:8; 21:6). The beatitude that follows, "Blessed are they who wash their robes . . ." (22:14), is most likely a recollection of 7:14, in which the angel explains to John the identity of the 144,000. The "tree of life" and the gates of the city are probably allusions to the vision of the New Jerusalem (21:24-27; 22:2). The saying about "dogs, the sorcerers, the unchaste . . . and all who love and practice deceit" (22:15) recalls those who are not allowed into the New Jerusalem, since it is the place where God and the Lamb reside (see 21:9, 27). It also suggests those who have made allegiance with the dragon and its beasts (see 13:6-8).

Jesus continues, providing further authentication for the book of Revelation, here called "testimony for the churches" (22:16). His authority to speak lies in the fact that he is the messiah: thus the reference to the root of David and the bright morning star (see Isa 11:1; Num 24:17).

The statement about the Spirit and the bride (22:17) has all the flavor of a call to worship, and some scholars have suggested that the author's liturgical allusion was intentional. The Spirit is the one who speaks to the churches through the prophets (see 2:7; 19:10). The bride is the New Jerusalem (see 21:2, 9). The one "who hears" is the one who reads and takes to heart the words of the book of Revelation. All say, "Come," addressed to the risen Jesus. He is the coming one. The invitation for the thirsty to come (22:17) is reminiscent of the promise made to the inhabitants of the New Jerusalem that they will have access to "the spring of life-giving water" (21:6).

The book ends with a warning to would-be editors not to add to, take away from, or otherwise alter the contents of this book (22:18).

Certainly such things happened because ancient religious documents were considered to be community expressions of faith and recollections of larger oral or written traditions. Therefore, if a scribe found that something was missing or thought that a clarification of meaning was necessary, he would simply make the change. However, this warning might also serve to assure the reader that the content of the book is reliable, much like the statements of authenticity we have seen throughout this section. See, for example, 22:7, 12, and 20. In sum, whatever the involvement of the human author, the book of Revelation is reliable because God is its source (see 1:1).

Once again Jesus promises, "I am coming soon!" (22:20), to which the author, on behalf of the readers, answers, "Amen," meaning, "So be it." Certainly this is a message of hope for the persecuted! However, the time is *coming*; it is not yet here. Therefore the author adds a prayer of petition, "Come, Lord Jesus" (in Aramaic *marana tha*).

Finally, the book ends as it began—with literary features of a letter. Thus we see a closing greeting, wishing the grace (i.e., gift) of Jesus on all (22:21). Amen. So be it!

 Prayer starter: In the last chapter of Revelation, Jesus promises three times that he is coming soon (22:7, 12, 20). What does this mean to you? What do you believe about Jesus' return? Reflect on Jesus' promise: "I am coming soon." After some time of reflection, if you can, respond: "Come, Lord Jesus!" (Rev 22:20).

EXPLORING LESSON SEVEN

1. Both the bride and the wedding day of the Lamb are used as metaphors (19:7-8). What do they symbolize? (See 21:2; Matt 22:1-14; 25:1-13.)

_____

_____

_____

_____

_____

2. What is the meaning of the word "Alleluia" (19:1, 3, 4, 6)? (See 1 Chron 16:36; Ps 150.)

_____

_____

_____

_____

_____

3. John is told to worship God, not the angel (19:10). How might we understand this warning in our own lives? How can even good things or people distract us from God if we become too focused on them?

_____

_____

_____

_____

_____

4. The rider (the risen Christ) is called "Faithful and True," "Word of God," and "King of kings and Lord of lords" (19:11-16; 3:14). Which of these titles leads you most meaningfully into prayer? Why?

_____

_____

_____

_____

_____

5. As he often does in Revelation, John borrows from apocalyptic literature in Ezekiel to describe "God's great feast." Compare the feast described in Ezekiel 39:17-20 with the wedding feast in Revelation 19:17-18. Why do you think John uses this violent imagery?

_____

_____

_____

_____

6. a) More destruction by the Devil occurs in 20:7-10. Discuss the source of John's reference to Gog, the King, and Magog. (See Ezek 38:1–39:20.)

_____

_____

_____

_____

   b) What is John trying to say to his readers?

_____

_____

_____

_____

7. "All the dead were judged according to their deeds" (20:13). Do you fear divine judgment? By which attitudes, behaviors, and actions do you hope to be judged?

_____

_____

_____

_____

8. There is no need for a temple in the new Jerusalem (21:22-24). Why?

_____

_____

_____

_____

_____

9. Jesus promises that he is "coming soon" (22:7, 12, 20). Almost two thousand years have passed since these words were written. What does "soon" mean to you?

_____

_____

_____

_____

_____

10. a) Now that you have completed your study of the book of Revelation, think back on your impression of the book before you began. Has your understanding of the purpose or message of Revelation changed? In what way?

_____

_____

_____

_____

   b) What message from the book of Revelation or what new information from this study will stay with you going forward?

_____

_____

_____

_____

CLOSING PRAYER

Prayer

Blessed are they who wash their robes so as to have the right to the tree of life and enter the city through its gates. (Rev 22:14)

Jesus, Lamb of God, return to us soon and lead us triumphantly through the gates of your heavenly city. As we wait patiently and expectantly for that time to come, help us to serve you alone, following your command to love God and neighbor, recognizing you as our Beginning and End. As our time together studying your Word comes to a close, we pray for one another, especially . . .

PRAYING WITH YOUR GROUP

Because we know that the Bible allows us to hear God's voice, prayer provides the context for our study and sharing. By speaking and listening to God and each other, the discussion often grows to more deeply bond us to one another and to God.

At *the beginning and end of each lesson* simple prayers are provided for individual use, and also may be used within the group setting. Most of the closing prayers provided with each lesson relate directly to a theme from that lesson and encourage you to pray together for people and events in your local community.

Of course, there are many ways to center ourselves in God's presence as we gather together in groups around the word of God. We provide some additional suggestions here knowing you and your group will make prayer a priority as part of your gathering. These are simply alternative ways to pray if your group would like to try something different from those prayers provided in the previous pages.

Conversational Prayer

This form of prayer allows for the group members to pray in their own words in a way that is not intimidating. The group leader begins with Step One, inviting all to focus on the presence of Christ among them. After a few moments of quiet, the group leader invites anyone in the group to voice a prayer or two of thanksgiving; once that is complete, then anyone who has personal intentions may pray in their own words for their needs; finally, the group prays for the needs of others.

A suggested process:
In your own words, speak simple and short prayers to allow time for others to add their voices.

Focus on one "step" at a time, not worrying about praying for everything in your mental list at once.

Step One	Visualize Christ. Welcome him.
	Imagine him present with you in your group.
	Allow time for some silence.
Step Two	Gratitude opens our hearts.
	Use simple words such as, "Thank you, Lord, for . . ."
Step Three	Pray for your own needs knowing that others will pray with you.
	Be specific and honest.
	Use "I" and "me" language.

Step Four	Pray for others by name, with love.
	You may voice your agreement ("Yes, Lord").
	End with gratitude for sharing concerns.

Praying Like Ignatius

St. Ignatius Loyola, whose life and ministry are the foundation of the Jesuit community, invites us to enter into Scripture texts in order to experience the scenes, especially scenes of the gospels or other narrative parts of Scripture. Simply put, this is a method of creatively imagining the scene, viewing it from the inside, and asking God to meet you there. Most often, this is a personal form of prayer, but in a group setting, some of its elements can be helpful if you allow time for this process.

A suggested process:

- Select a scene from the chapters in the particular lesson.
- Read that scene out loud in the group, followed by some quiet time.
- Ask group members to place themselves in the scene (as a character, or as an onlooker) so that they can imagine the emotions, responses, and thinking that may have taken place. Notice the details and the tone, and imagine the interaction with the Lord that is taking place.
- Share with the group any insights that came to you in this quiet imagining.
- Allow each person in the group to thank God for some insight and to pray about some request that may have surfaced.

Sacred Reading (or Lectio Divina)

This method of prayer invites us to "listen with the ear of the heart" as St. Benedict's rule would say. We listen to the words and the phrasing, asking God to speak to our innermost being. Again, this method of prayer is most often used in an individual setting but may also be used in an adapted way within a group.

A suggested process:

- Select a scene from the chapters in the particular lesson.
- Read the scene out loud in the group, perhaps two times.
- Ask group members to ponder a word or phrase that stands out to them.
- The group members could then simply speak the word or phrase as a kind of litany of what was meaningful for your group.
- Allow time for more silence to ponder the words that were heard, asking God to reveal to you what message you are meant to hear, how God is speaking to you.
- Follow up with spoken intentions at the close of this group time.

REFLECTING ON SCRIPTURE

Reading Scripture is an opportunity not simply to learn new information but to listen to God who loves you. Pray that the same Holy Spirit who guided the formation of Scripture will inspire you to correctly understand what you read, and empower you to make what you read a part of your life.

The inspired word of God contains layers of meaning. As you make your way through passages of Scripture, whether studying a book of the Bible or focusing on a biblical theme, you may find it helpful to ask yourself these four questions:

What does the Scripture passage say?
Read the passage slowly and reflectively. Become familiar with it. If the passage you are reading is a narrative, carefully observe the characters and the plot. Use your imagination to picture the scene or enter into it.

What does the Scripture passage mean?
Read the footnotes in your Bible and the commentary provided to help you understand what the sacred writers intended and what God wants to communicate by means of their words.

What does the Scripture passage mean to me?
Meditate on the passage. God's word is living and powerful. What is God saying to you? How does the Scripture passage apply to your life today?

What am I going to do about it?
Try to discover how God may be challenging you in this passage. An encounter with God contains a challenge to know God's will and follow it more closely in daily life. Ask the Holy Spirit to inspire not only your mind but your life with this living word.